5 Routes to TRENT

by Roderick Fowkes

Copyright Book Law Publications – First published in the United Kingdom in 2016

ISBN 978-1-909625-63-1

Printed and bound by The Amadeus Press, Cleckheaton, West Yorkshire
Published by Book Law Publications, 382 Carlton Hill, Nottingham, NG4 1JA

Front Cover : What were these two Electro-diesels doing at Trent station?
Answer – see page 90!

Back Cover : Trent, a station without a town.
Trent station was last century some might say, one of the cornerstones of the Midland Railway Empire. Of Midland Gothic architecture with its honeycomb of cellars and interlinking upper storeys, Trent's position and importance as an interchange junction for five main railway routes, through the plethora of junctions, served London, Birmingham, Derby, Chesterfield and Nottingham. Remarkably enough, trains could depart from opposite platforms in opposite directions to the same destination.

CONTENTS

Five Routes to Trent

The plethora of junctions around Trent was principally created in the thirty years from 1839, when in that summer; the Midland Counties Railway opened its line from Derby to Nottingham to passenger traffic with four intermediate stations at Borrowash, Breaston, Long Eaton and Beeston, with Spondon opening later that year. To avoid confusion with Beeston, the station at Breaston was re-named Sawley in 1840 – my grandfather was the stationmaster there when it closed in 1930. Also in 1840, the company's extension south to Leicester was completed. In 1844, the company amalgamated with the Birmingham & Derby Junction Railway and the North Midland Railway to form the Midland Railway, with Derby as its headquarters. Three years later, the Erewash Valley line was opened, and finally, the branch line to Stenson Junction providing the connection to Birmingham was instituted in 1873.

Further stations on the Derby-Nottingham line were opened, Draycott in 1852, Attenborough in 1864, and Sawley Junction in December 1888. With new junctions and the rearrangement of the layout of lines in the vicinity, a station called simply Trent was opened on 1st May 1862 - but its original purpose was not to serve Long Eaton, that already had a station at Meadow Lane, which when closed and demolished later moved to a more central position in the town. The direct line from there to Platt's crossing becoming Trent girder yard, with the truncated line from Sawley Junction re-aligned to connect at Trent Station North Junction.

Who could argue with the adage that school days are the best times of your life? No sooner had we trooped in for morning assembly when, just over a quarter of a mile away, a 'Jubilee' would rattle by at 9.10am with an express for London. Scant regard was paid to the music teacher when the lunchtime freight from Toton to Chaddesden went by hauled by a Beyer-Garratt 2-6-6-2T. All trains heading towards Derby, except those via Way & Works, whistled a routing at Sawley Crossing and these could clearly be heard. The Chaddesden freight trundled past with an endless stream of wagons, to be followed in the opposite direction by another 'Jubilee'-hauled express for St Pancras.

I was born in Breaston, a village midway between Derby and Nottingham, two miles from the largest marshalling yard in Britain – Toton. Unauthorised incursion into Toton MPD (18A) on Sunday afternoons was commonplace, the huge depot with its three roundhouses, Nos. 2&3 housing a longitudinal inside through road for the mighty Beyer-Garratt locomotives, had an eerie perception about them. Inside the sheds steam engines stood forlorn looking, some with their smoke box doors open, others receiving attention but not on this day, the requisite 'Not to be moved' boards in position. These majestic machines stood silent, a few awaiting the arrival of the 'steam raiser' with his supply of firelighters, in readiness for work on Monday morning.

Like so many boys of my generation, I wanted to be an engine driver; my dreams however were dashed in 1956 when I went for a medical at Derby. Some forty-hours later the caller-up from Toton was the bringer of bad news. I had not attained the required colour vision level and therefore was unsuitable for the footplate grade. This was truly the darkest period I had known. I probably wept at the time. The consolation of being offered a position of Junior Porter, which at the time was not taken up, was of little consequence.

In spite of this disappointment, some five months later help was at hand and it came in the form of George Mellors, a porter at Draycott and Breaston station. George had kept me in touch with local developments. A likeable fellow he was renowned for his rendering of 'Draycott' in his high-pitched falsetto voice when a train arrived at the station. He also rode the station bicycle in a very uncertain manner when delivering parcels between trains. One day he was showing me how to knock the crank of my bicycle back into shape when he mentioned that there was a vacancy at Trent for a Junior Porter, a position I had earlier turned down. This opportunity could not be allowed to pass; I applied for the job, was successful and began my 39-year career with British Railways on January 14 1957. I reported to A.W. (Tony) Smith the stationmaster; he explained the role of Junior Porter general-purpose relief, rate of pay 63 shillings per week and the signalboxes at which I would be relieving. Early in 1960 and with no ambition to be a signalman, I undertook a clerical examination and moved to Trent station as a Telegraph Clerk.

Sir Edmund Beckett, who in the 19th century was closely connected with the birth of independent railway companies, wrote of Trent: "You arrive at Trent, but where that is I cannot tell. I suppose it is somewhere near the River Trent; but then the Trent is a very long river. You get out of your train to obtain refreshments, and having taken them you endeavour to find your train and your carriage. But whether it is on this side or that, and whether it is going north or south, this way or that, you cannot tell. Bewildered, you frantically rush into your carriage; the train moves off round a curve; then you are horrified to see some red lights glaring in front of, and you are in imminent expectation of a collision when your fellow passengers calm your fears by telling you that they are only the tail lamps of your own train!"

Further to the Baron's comments, "Well, I'll go to Trent", was an expression that my mother would make when she was faced with situations surpassing belief. Trent was a station without a town, 119¾ miles from London (St Pancras) on the former Midland Railway lines of the London Midland Region of British Railways. Sited in the south-east corner of Derbyshire, the county town was situated just over nine miles to the west, and Nottingham just under seven miles to the east. The River Trent, third longest river in England, from which the station took its name, runs nearby. Trent station was last century some might say, one of the cornerstones of the Midland Railway Empire. Of Midland Railway Gothic architecture with its honeycomb of cellars and interlinking upper storeys, Trent's position and importance as an interchange junction for five main railway routes, through the superabundance of junctions, serving Nottingham, Derby, Birmingham, Chesterfield and the City of London. Remarkably enough, trains could depart from opposite platforms in opposite directions to the same destination.

The station was a sizeable one with its single island platform, included booking hall, waiting rooms, refreshment room, bookstall, train crew relief cabin, and a ticket barrier that was manned on the early and late turns. This issued either a platform ticket, or a ticket to purchase a ticket to travel at the booking office. The Signal & Telegraph department had a room at platform level, whilst the Permanent Way Inspector's office was located upstairs. The station site was only surrounded only by an isolated farm, a cottage that was linked to a rifle range, the Stationmaster's house, and also ten railway cottages. With no buses passing the station entrance, and no taxi rank, many would-be passengers opted for 'Shank's pony' as a means of getting to the station, either by using the 600 yards of sparsely gas-lit footpath from North Erewash Junction, or by the longer route down Meadow Lane and over Long Eaton Junction level crossing.

Each day nearly 100 passenger and parcels trains called at Trent station, with very few passenger trains not stopping there. Local services were in the hands of ex-Midland Class '2P' & '4P' 4-4-0s or Fowler and Stanier 2-6-4Ts, supplemented by the odd Class '4F' 0-6-0 with archaic non-corridor coaches on workmens' services, those then giving way to diesel-multiple-units operating between Derby, Nottingham and Lincoln, as well as between Nottingham, Leicester and Birmingham. The two routes connected at Trent to provide an interval service between Derby and Leicester that supplemented the Manchester to London (St Pancras) expresses. The principle expresses from St Pancras, those to Manchester, generally avoided running via Trent station, whilst the services to Leeds and Bradford, and also 'The Thames-Clyde Express', were routed through the station, initially to eschew the conurbations of Derby and Nottingham, from where connecting services were in place for the transfer of passengers.

At the turn of the century there were two rows of trees on each side of the station, and those on the north side are extant today, despite the remodelling of the junction when the station closed from New Year's Day 1968 and the building of an adjacent industrial estate, whilst those on the south side were felled to allow the construction of the high-level goods lines into Toton. These allowed the intensive goods workings to avoid Trent station and also the two busy level crossings in later years on the Erewash Valley line at Long Eaton; the high-level lines carried the heaviest freight traffic in the country and remain in use today.

In the early 1950s, much to the delight of trainspotters, there was an Anglo-Scottish transfer of half a dozen long serving Stanier 'Jubilees' between the Midland Division and Carlisle (Kingmoor), Perth and Glasgow sheds. Other unusual visitors would be locomotives for overhaul at Derby Locomotive Works, which would include those from Plaistow shed in East London, these often finding their way to Derby Works dead in a freight train from Wellingborough.

In addition, locomotives just out-shopped would often have a trial run from Derby to Trent via the North Curve and back; conveniently, the use of the Sawley Junction – Trent Station North Junction – Trent Station South Junction – Sheet Stores Junction – Sawley Junction 'circular' route negated any need to run-round any stock on a loaded test run. In 1954, the first lightweight diesel railcar emerged from the Litchurch Lane Works in Derby and, over the next five years, 1,000 such vehicles would be turned out. A programme of driver training - handling - was undertaken between Leek and Rocester using the Churnet Valley branch line, the diesel-multiple-units returning in the afternoon to the Carriage & Wagon Works after running to Trent via Chaddesden and the North Curve.

I was brought up on a diet of 'Jubilee' and Stanier and later BR Standard Class '5' 4-6-0 locomotives from depots at Millhouses (Sheffield) shed, Holbeck (Leeds), Trafford Park (Manchester), Kentish Town (London), Derby and Nottingham, as they were the usual first-line of motive power on the expresses running to and from St Pancras. Freight traffic was handled by Stanier 2-8-0s and the mighty Beyer-Garratts that were soon to be ousted by the introduction of BR Standard 2-10-0 Class '9Fs'. There was also the odd WD 'Austerity', plus the multitude of Midland Railway-designed 0-6-0s, many of which lasted almost until the end of steam in the area.

Amongst the variations was the daily working of 'Patriot' No. 45509 *The Derbyshire Yeomanry*, which for a brief spell was allocated to Derby shed and regularly worked the 7.35am Nottingham to Bristol service. A Holbeck-engine appeared on the afternoon Cricklewood to Derby (St Mary's) working, en route to Carlisle with milk empties, whilst a Fowler '4F' 0-6-0 invariably worked the evening lettuce train. One freight that often produced a locomotive from north of the border was the 4.25pm Class 'C' Leicester to Carlisle fully-fitted freight - often referred to as the 'Boxer' - the engine being a 'Jubilee' or Stanier '5MT' with the (St Rollox) enlarged numerals. Another working that occasionally produced a Glasgow-allocated 'Jubilee' was a Sunday afternoon filling-in turn on a local Derby to Nottingham passenger train, which returned later in the evening.

A feature of the Midland Division operation was double-heading, where, south of Derby and Nottingham, pre-war speeds had been fully restored, but with increased loads. A limit of 300 tons tare weight was fixed for 'Jubilee' on 'XL Limit' timings, but unfortunately though a nine-coach train of standard stock, including a restaurant car, exceeded this figure, so a pilot could be called for by the driver of a 'Jubilee' as well as a 'Black Five' if he was expected to keep time on this schedule. With a Class '2P' or '4P' 4-4-0 as the pilot engine, one did wonder at times whether this was a hindrance or a help.

In 1955 'Royal Scot' No. 46120 *Royal Iniskilling Fusilier* had been on loan for twelve weeks to the Mechanical & Electrical Engineers department at Derby, from where its chief duties were the 7.55am Derby to London (St Pancras) service and the 5.30pm St Pancras to Nottingham duty. This may well have been the prelude to the transfer of six 'Royal Scots' from the Western Division for the 1957 winter timetable. Allocated to Kentish Town (14B), Nos. 46110 *Grenadier Guardsman*, 46116 *Irish Guardsman*, 46131 *The Royal Warwickshire Regiment*, 46152 *The King's Dragoon Guardsman*, and 46157 *The Royal Artilleryman* were put to work on the Manchester route. On 'XL Limit' schedules the 'Royal Scots' were allowed 300 tons between Derby and Manchester, whilst 340 tons applied elsewhere. This effectively reduced the uneconomic double-heading on the Midland main line.

A popular haunt where I spent many happy hours was Trent Lock, often referred to as 'Bunker', just to the south of Trent station where the river is crossed. It was a busy location on a summer Sunday evening, and even more so in the week when there was the often-endless procession of mineral trains from Toton rattling by on the high-level goods line to the Stewarts & Lloyds' steelworks at Corby, and also to Wellingborough and Brent, where London had an insatiable appetite for coal.

Situated between Trent Junction Signal Box and Red Hill Tunnel, it was nearly an ideal spot for viewing trains as the only ones that did not pass there were those from Derby towards Trent, or off the route from Stenson Junction. Looking north from the tunnel towards Trent, the left-hand pair of lines were the original ones of 1840 – the main line from Leicester for Derby and Nottingham – with the 1893-built freight route being on the east side. Interestingly, with over fifty years between the creation of each pair of lines, the Trent viaduct had differing styles, while the original tunnel through Red Hill was sixteen yards shorter than its younger neighbour – 154 yards as opposed to 170 yards. Unfortunately, anyone choosing this location to watch trains on weekdays could miss out badly as there was a considerable amount of freight traffic to and from the Castle Donington branch, and that would be too distant to record. In fact there was no perfect location to see everything, as if trainspotters positioned themselves on Trent station, with the requisite platform ticket, they would miss out on the expresses between St Pancras and Manchester, which would pass just half a mile away as they sped between Trent Junction and Sheet Stores Junction.

The coal trains from Toton, and those returning empty wagons to Toton and Beeston ran throughout the day and night. Stone trains operated during the day from the Northamptonshire ore fields, most having loose-coupled iron-ore tippler wagons that were not vacuum-fitted. These trains were worked by Stanier '8Fs' and the renowned Beyer-Garratts before the advent of the '9Fs'. Services of note were Ashwell to Frodingham, Corby to Glazebrook, Glendon to Burslem, Storefield to York and Wellingborough to Grange. The returning empties were worked back on the 7.30am Toton to Pain's Siding, and the duty from Clay Cross to Wellingborough. Most Monday mornings would see a cavalcade of five locomotives coupled together, all in steam, that were running from the Birmingham Division sheds of Saltley and Bescot to reach Toton. When the original ten 'Peak' diesels were displaced off the Western Lines and allocated to Toton for freight workings in 1962, a brake-tender was often used to provide additional brakeforce.

The periodic shipment of Spanish ore was guaranteed to provide a varied selection of motive power from depots in the north-west. This commodity was extremely heavy and each train was limited to twenty-six non-fitted iron ore wagons; they ran from Birkenhead via Crewe and the North Stafford route and over the Castle Donington line to Sheet Stores Junction, Trent and the Erewash Valley to Stanton Gate for the British Steel Corporation Works. This influx of locomotives on the unbalanced workings supplemented Toton's allocation at the time.

Interrupting the flow of the River Trent on its way out into the North Sea through the East Midlands were two weirs, within a mile of each other. The first was at nearby Sawley, just downstream of the confluence of the River Derwent, whilst the other one was located near to Trent Lock, close to its meeting point with the River Soar. When this weir inextricably burst in 1953 it undermined the abutments of the viaduct that carried the goods lines, and subsequently boulders had to be unloaded from rail vehicles to consolidate the footings.

Quite unexpectedly, during the mid-1950s five Lincoln-allocated former Great Central Railway 'D11' class 4-4-0s began to work through to the Midland lines. The former Midland shed at Lincoln had come under the control of the Eastern Region and, although a small number of London Midland Region engines were still serviced there, most of the through workings between Lincoln and Derby were in the hands of Eastern Region locomotives. In the spring of 1957, five 'D16' class 4-4-0s from Cambridge replaced the 'D11s', which were transferred to Sheffield (Darnall) shed. However, that proved to be a temporary measure as a year later the 'D16s' were themselves replaced by the introduction of diesel-multiple-units on the Derby to Lincoln, Leicester and Nottingham services. Other unusual visitors to Trent would be locomotives for overhaul at Derby Works, which would include those from Plaistow shed in East London, these often finding their way to the Derby Works dead in a freight train from Brent to Wellingborough and Chaddesden.

A further reshuffle of express motive power took place in July 1958 when six 'Britannia' Pacifics, Nos. 70004 *William Shakespeare* and 70014 *Iron Duke* from Stewarts Lane, 70015 *Apollo*, 70017 *Arrow*, and 70021 *Morning Star* from Cardiff (Canton), and 70042 *Lord Roberts* from Stratford were procured and transferred to the Midland Division and allocated to Trafford Park, Nos. 70004, 70014, 70017 and 70042 initially stopping off at Kentish Town shed for a couple of weeks. This allowed the 'Royal Scots' to be returned from Kentish Town to the Western Division. Three more 'Britannias', Nos. 70031 *Byron*, 70032 *Tennyson* and 70033 *Charles Dickens*, appeared at a later date, bringing the stud of 'Britannias' at Trafford Park to nine.

Although freight trains had timetabled paths in the same way as passenger and parcels trains, bad weather conditions often hindered their progress. Fog was a prime cause of delay, particularly whenever double-block working had to be resorted to in the absence of fogsignalmen. Fog in those days was, 'a three-way killer with no holds barred'. 'It chokes you. It chills you. It blinds you', potent in the extreme for the elderly and those with breathing difficulties. The old fashioned pea-soupers did not lift for days on end and it blanketed all sounds so that an approaching train could barely be heard until it arrived in the platform. Most freight trains that had commenced their journey at Toton, Beeston, Nottingham and Chaddesden could be expected to run reasonably near to their booked time, whilst empty wagon trains from various locations often ran late and had to take their chance with others. Express freight services running under Class 'C' headcodes, as well as partially-fitted ones with 'D' and 'E' headcodes, were generally good timekeepers.

If the signalman was not careful he could create an impasse at Trent Station South Junction. Unlikely as that might seem, it actually happened, although not through any lack of co-operation between the signalmen. A freight train for the Castle Donington branch had been accepted from Trent Station North Junction. Meanwhile, the signalman at Trent South had a freight signalled for Toton coming from Trent Junction and it was routed along the platform line to Trent North. All very well, but when this train arrived at Trent North it was realised that it had been wrongly described and should have gone to Beeston. As a result of this direction error neither train was able to move forward along the proper route. One or other would have to advance a sufficient distance to allow the other train to pass, and then the first train would need to reverse to take its intended route, a time-consuming exercise with possibly sixty or so wagons in tow.

The nightly Ancoats to London Class 'C' fully-fitted train often produced one of the four named Stanier 'Black Fives', two of which were transferred to Newton Heath from St Rollox shed in Glasgow, still sporting their enlarged numerals. It was the only freight train other than the 'Sheet Stores trip' to be booked via the North Curve from Sawiey Junction and this routing effected relief by a Toton train crew at Trent station. Unfortunately, for those of the train spotting fraternity, the fast freights ran during the night, except the Leicester to Carlisle and Somers Town to Masborough services. The nocturnal fitted freights would include the Attercliffe to Birmingham, Carlisle to Leicester, Carlton to Leicester, Dringhouses to Lawley Street, Edge Hill to Nottingham, the Glasgow (Buchanan Street) to London (St Pancras), Luton to Bathgate (motor cars), Greenhill-Wilhampstead (returning empties), Hurlford to Brent, Moston to Brent, Nottingham to Bristol, Rowsley to London, Stourton to St Pancras, and the Carlisle to Cricklewood Milk (466) with its Holbeck 'Jubilee' – notably, the latter working had regulation preference over the 9.30pm Bradford Forster Square to London express through Trent Junction.

Enginemen and guards were conveyed between Toton to Trent station by a crew bus, and it was not unusual for Nottingham Control Office to ring up asking to intercept a train crew. They might have been travelling to Kettering or Wellingborough to work a Down freight train when it was learnt that it was not running. Many of the goods trains from the south - apart from the empties from the London area - emanated from the ore fields in Northamptonshire. When Toton Yard was on the block, which was quite often, the stone trains, regarded as through workings, were turned out at Ratcliffe Junction - just south of Red Hill Tunnel - or Trent Junction to run through Trent station and along the Erewash Valley, instead of standing on the Down high-level goods line behind other freight trains that were awaiting acceptance into Toton marshalling yard.

Trent station could be a most inhospitable place, with its biting north-north- easterly winds chilling the bone to the marrow. Tom Blakeman, with his wife and three daughters ran the refreshment room. It was never particularly busy, although no doubt much appreciated by passengers subjected to late-running services or severed connections, the hardiest of individuals seeking solace in the refreshment room, when open. The station bookstall, still open in the mid-1950s, had long since disappeared by my arrival at Trent.

One of the biggest problems at the station was whether to hold trains for connection in the event of late running, bearing in mind that a connection maintained at Trent may result in another being missed elsewhere. The Divisional Manager, Nottingham, issued guidelines in the form of 'Detention of Trains for Connection at Trent'. The station was manned with a foreman on each shift, two porters on early and late turn, supplemented by a parcels porter, with one porter on the night turn, the ticket barrier being staffed on the early and late turns. The station foreman was also responsible for sorting the Special Traffic Notices at Trent and for arranging their distribution to the local signal boxes. Few options were available in getting them to outlying locations, the lamp man being utilised occasionally. On Fridays (pay day) they would be given to the respective signalmen, and most were handed to the guard of a passenger train to throw them out when passing the signal boxes, which would have been advised of their expectance in advance.

At Trent Junction the train would not have been going too fast, nor at Sheet Stores with its permanent speed restriction over the junction, but beyond the tunnel, Ratcliffe Junction Signal Box, however, was different as the train would now be well into its stride. With trains often passing on the Down and Up goods lines at the same time, this hindered the delivery, and it was not unknown for the notices to land in a coal wagon bound for Brent yard! The prevailing wind and a poor aim from the guard could also result in recovery of these from an adjacent cornfield.

Over the years Trent won many awards. For example in 1953 it gained a first prize for cleanliness and a third prize for its gardens. Although not widely known, all manner of Royalty often visited Trent, which was possibly unbeknown to them, albeit in the form of the Royal train that stabled overnight between Trent Station North Junction and Sawley Junction - the North Curve. On one such occasion I was on a night turn as a telegraph clerk in May 1964. That night's platform activity saw a portion detached off the rear of the 11.50pm London (St Pancras) to Leeds (City) train, which was hauled by a brace of splendidly turned out BR Sulzer 'Type 2' diesels, Nos. D7588 and D7589. 'Black Five' No. 44918 then hauled the detachment on to the North Curve for stabling, whilst another 'Black Five' No. 45464 was attached on the rear. Special instructions were issued on 'a need to know basis' in connection with the working of Royal trains and these were given code words – 'Grove' was used when the Reigning Monarch was aboard, and 'Deepdene' for other members of the Royal family. Other well-known celebrities would also change trains at Trent; amongst those mentioned by signalman George Bailey was Ella Fitzgerald, and on one occasion I saw Primo Carnera.

Quite often, a somewhat liberal view was taken of the low 15mph permanent speed restriction through the platform by some trains, on the Down road in particular, and none more so than the Luton to Bathgate motor car train and the 'Condor', with its 27 roller-bearing fitted, vacuum-braked 'Platefit' wagons loaded with containers, these making staccato overtures on the jointed track. Another train that often showed scant regard for the mandatory speed restriction was the Down 'Thames-Clyde Express' until a station stop was introduced in late 1962. During the summer months a relief train ran from Glasgow (St Enoch) to London (St Pancras) on Mondays, Fridays and Saturdays, starting some thirty minutes ahead of the 'Thames-Clyde Express'. In the reverse direction, a relief train ran as far as Sheffield on Mondays, Fridays and Saturdays, and this was extended to Glasgow on peak Summer Saturdays.

Another long distance express was the 7.00am Cleethorpes to Birmingham (New Street) service, which was hauled by an Eastern Region 'B1' class 4-6-0 that returned with the afternoon working. In the late 1950s the train was extended to Bournemouth on a Summer Saturday, and in the early 1960s it conveyed through coaches for Sidmouth and Exmouth. An overnight Leeds to Bedford parcels train detached its rearmost van in the Up platform just after half-past three, to be picked up within the hour by the 3.57am Derby to Nottingham parcels duty. During the time that the van occupied the platform line other trains were routed through the third Up passenger line.

Motive power was ever changing - late 1959 saw a further batch of '7P' 4-6-0s obtained from the Western Lines by the Midland, with rebuilt 'Patriots' and 'Royal Scots' allocated to Kentish Town, Millhouses and Nottingham. The latter two sheds received their first '7Ps', and these included No. 46100 *Royal Scot* and the appropriately named No. 46112 *Sherwood Forester* exchanged with Holbeck for Kentish Town's No.

46130, no doubt with a view to it working the 'Robin Hood' - the 8.15am Up service from Nottingham and the corresponding 4.45pm return duty from St Pancras.

Towards the end of 1960 Trafford Park relinquished its 'Britannias' back to the Western Lines as these engines had not taken kindly to regular service over the curves on the Midland, in particular the Derby to Manchester route. Main line diesels were also appearing in ever increasing numbers, and not only from BR Workshops. The Metropolitan-Vickers 'Type 2' Co-Bo 1,200hp units, with a top speed of 75mph, had a short spell operating in pairs on the St Pancras to Manchester (Central) expresses. Also coming on stream around this time were BR/Sulzer 'Type 4' diesels, and it wouldn't be long before they would monopolise the working of the expresses on the Midland main line, something they would continue to do until the introduction of HSTs in 1982.

In December 1960, after some wet weather the swollen River Erewash washed away a culvert at Attenborough Junction on the Derby to Nottingham line, which remained closed for the next five days. Throughout this period the Derby to Nottingham diesel-multiple-unit service was diverted to Leicester using the North Curve at Trent, with a bus service affording connections between Sawley Junction and Attenborough. In addition, a special bus service operated between Derby's Midland station and Derby (Friargate) to connect into the ex-Great Northern route trains to Nottingham (Victoria). Other trains were diverted from Nottingham to run via Radford and Trowell, where a diesel-multiple-unit ran shuttle services to and from Long Eaton. A couple of particularly unusual workings involved the 4.55pm Birmingham to Cleethorpes service, with a Thompson 'B1' class 4-6-0 taking the Erewash Valley route as far as Trowell, where another 'B1' attached to the rear and continued via Radford to reach Nottingham. Similarly, the 8.01pm Mail service from Lincoln to Tamworth was diverted over the Trowell branch, but it then ran via Butterley, Ambergate and Derby.

Seven years after its opening, Trent station was the scene of one of the worst railway disasters in the history of the Midland Railway. An excursion train returning from Nottingham Goose Fair had been stopped outside the station when it was struck from the rear by the Night Mail express; nine passengers were killed.

Trent Station ultimately died quietly on New Year's Eve 1967. There had never been ranks of taxicabs outside, no buses passing the entrance, or no tannoys to disturb the tranquil surroundings. It was situated in a truly idyllic rural location without civilization on the doorstep, and many no doubt enjoyed this charm, but for me it would always be particularly special as it was the location where my 39 year career with British Railways began on 14 January 1957 after being interviewed by the then Stationmaster, Mr A. W. Smith, for the position of junior porter general-purpose relief. I spent six years there as a Telegraph & Booking Clerk, on reflection perhaps too long but nonetheless an enjoyable experience.

Special thanks go to Joe Wade and Tony Smith for providing photographs from their own collections to supplement those of my own. I am also indebted to David Allen for allowing me the opportunity to share with you this compilation of pictures

Roderick H Fowkes

Tony Smith took this photograph, circa 1960, probably from off the corbal table in the castellated turret of the goods line tunnel at Red Hill. Pictured here on the main line viaduct over the River Trent, about to enter Red Hill tunnel is Metropolitan-Vickers 'Type 2' Co-Bo 1,200hp diesels (D5702 leading) working a Manchester (Central) to London (St Pancras) express. Introduced in 1958, and with a top speed of 75mph, all twenty were initially allocated to the Midland Lines, and could also be found operating in pairs working BRs fastest freight train named 'Condor' from London's Hendon and Glasgow's Gushetfaulds goods depots. *Tony Smith.*

Trent Lock was a favourite 'spotting' location to watch the many trains passing on the multi-tracks here from various locations – both passenger and freight. A leisure pursuit for many at the weekends, the railway location often being referred to as 'Bunker'. The view is looking south towards Red Hill across the viaducts over the River Trent and taken on 26 July 1956. The main line tunnel through Red Hill is 154 yards in length, with the slightly longer goods line tunnel on the left that is 170 yards long. *Tony Smith.*

A scene of the River Trent Viaduct from Red Hill Tunnel on 14 July 1958, with Trent Junction signal box just visible. Trent Junction was where the Derby line diverged from the routes towards Trent station for the Erewash Valley or Nottingham. In this picture the signals indicate that Stanier 2-8-0 Class '8F' No. 48350 is taking its Beeston to Leicester coal train for a main line run, instead of being turned onto the goods line at Ratcliffe Junction, which is beyond the tunnel. Built in 1944 at Horwich Works and withdrawn in September 1967 from Trafford Park shed and cut up at Cashmore's, Newport. There was usually a constant procession of freight trains over the goods lines, but with nothing in sight there could be a problem, especially if that is a member of the permanent way staff on the goods line viaduct. *Tony Smith.*

Emerging from Red Hill tunnel approaching Ratcliffe Junction on the main line with steam to spare is Midland 0-6-0 Class '4F' No. 44223 of Leicester shed, working back home with a mineral train from Beeston Sidings on 3 May 1959. Built in 1926 at Derby Works and withdrawn in November 1963 from Nottingham shed and disposed of at Cashmore's, Great Bridge. *Tony Smith.*

An unidentified British Railways Standard 2-10-0 Class '9F' with a down freight from the south for Toton Yard approaching Red Hill tunnel on the goods line passing Ratcliffe Junction on 19 August 1958. *Tony Smith.*

Stanier 'Black Five' No. 44815 rumbles across the main line viaduct over the River Trent and is about to enter the 154 yards long Red Hill tunnel in May 1959 with a Beeston to Wellingborough mineral train. The signals indicate it will be turned onto the goods line at Ratcliffe Junction. Built in 1944 at Derby Works and withdrawn in February 1968 from Trafford Park shed and scrapped at Cohens, Kettering. *Tony Smith.*

Photographed from the castellated portal on the goods line of Red Hill tunnel in July 1959 is Eastern Region 'B1' No. 61374 with an abundance of steam working the 7.00am Cleethorpes to Birmingham express. Manufactured in 1951 by the North British Locomotive Company, Glasgow and withdrawn in September 1963 from Immingham shed and broken up at Cashmore's, Great Bridge. *Tony Smith.*

Immingham-allocated Thompson 'B1' No. 61318 has just left Trent station in July 1959 with the 7.00am Cleethorpes to Birmingham. Built in 1948 by North British Locomotive Company, Glasgow and withdrawn from Immingham shed in September 1963 and cut up at A. King & Sons Ltd. Norwich. The engine and coaches will leave Birmingham at 4.50pm in the afternoon returning to the East Coast resort. *Tony Smith.*

Passing Trent Junction in August 1958 and worked by Cravens 3-car unit is the 10.55am Nottingham to Leicester stopping train, the DMU service was inaugurated in April of that year. *Tony Smith.*

The 5.05pm London (St Pancras) to Bradford Forster Square has emerged from Red Hill tunnel, crossed the viaduct over the River Trent and the Cranfleet Cut and is about to pass Trent Junction signal box hauled by 'Jubilee' 4-6-0 Class '6P' No. 45557 *New Brunswick*. Built in 1934 by North British Locomotive Company, Glasgow and withdrawn in September 1964 from Derby shed and broken up at Cashmore's, Great Bridge. *Tony Smith.*

Midland 0-6-0 Class '4F' No. 44131 emerges from Red Hill New Tunnel in September 1960 with a southbound freight from Toton Yard. Built in 1925 at Crewe Works and withdrawn in November 1964 from Bury shed and broken up at T. W. Ward, Killamarsh in 1965. *Joe Wade.*

Johnson Midland design, rebuilt by Fowler from 1916 with non superheated Belpaire boiler is 0-6-0 Class '3F' No. 43751 a few miles south of Trent, unusually on the main line in Sutton Bonington cutting between Kegworth and Hathern in April 1958 working an up southbound mineral train. A 1901 build by Neilson & Co. and withdrawn from Sheffield (Grimesthorpe) shed in August 1961 and scrapped at Crewe Works. *Joe Wade.*

Owing to electrification work on the Western lines, certain Manchester (London Road) to London (Euston) expresses were diverted from Stoke-on-Trent over the North Stafford line to Stenson Junction; from there they took the branch line to Sheet Stores Junction and then up the Midland main line to St Pancras. This is the 12 noon from Manchester (London Road) hauled by a commendably clean Longsight 'Jubilee' 4-6-0 Class '6P' No. 45587 *Baroda* seen here accelerating away over Trent Junction in September 1960. Built in 1934 by North British Locomotive Co. Glasgow and withdrawn from Carnforth shed in December 1962 and scrapped at Horwich Works. *Joe Wade.*

'Jubilee' 4-6-0 Class '6P' No. 45602 *British Honduras* takes a breather over Trent Junction with a Manchester (Central) to London (St Pancras) express in June 1957. Manufactured in 1935 by North British Locomotive Company, Glasgow and withdrawn from Leeds (Holbeck) shed in April 1965 and disposed of at Drapers, Hull. *Joe Wade.*

Rebuilt 'Royal Scot' 4-6-0 Class '7P' No. 46152 *The King's Dragoon Guardsman* has just passed Sheet Stores Junction in January 1958 with a Manchester (Central) to London (St Pancras) express. The locomotive was one of six transferred from the Western Division and allocated to Kentish Town (14B) for the start of the 1957 winter timetable effectively reducing the uneconomic double-heading on the Midland Lines. Built in 1927 by North British Locomotive Company, Glasgow, supposedly, this was reputedly the original Royal Scot 6100, but swapped identities with 6152 in 1933 as a loco was required to tour North America and 6100 was not in the best of health. *Joe Wade.*

Under the shadow of the approaching introduction of diesel railcars, Fowler 2-6-4T Class '4MT' No. 42336 has just passed Trent Junction signal box heading a Nottingham-Leicester local train in June 1957 approaching the viaduct over the River Trent before entering Red Hill tunnel. Built in 1929 at Derby Works and withdrawn from Kentish Town shed in October 1962 and broken up at Crewe Works. The Nottingham to Leicester stopping service would be worked by diesel-multiple-units from the following spring. *Joe Wade.*

On its way home, Northampton-allocated Stanier LMS 2-8-0 Class '8F' No. 48305 crosses the viaduct over the River Trent on the Up goods line with a southbound freight from Toton Yard in June 1957. Built in 1943 at Crewe Works and withdrawn in 1968 from Speke Junction shed, fortunately it was rescued from Woodham's scrapyard in South Wales, the lifeline that saw it returned to steam at Loughborough on the preserved Great Central Railway. *Joe Wade.*

An unidentified Stanier 4-6-0 'Black Five' crossing the River Trent on the Up goods line and is about to enter Red Hill tunnel with a mixed train of empty carflats and covered vans from Greenhill to Wilhampstead in 1960. This was the return working of the Luton to Bathgate motorcar train. *Joe Wade.*

BR Standard 4-6-0 Class '5' No. 73067 accelerates away from Trent station in June 1957 with a Nottingham to London (St Pancras) semi-fast express. Built in 1954 at Crewe Works and withdrawn from Patricroft shed in March 1968 and cut up at Cashmore's, Great Bridge. There were doubts in some quarters as to whether they would match up to their Stanier counterparts and in practice proved that they could. *Joe Wade.*

First-generation Class 101 diesel multiple unit, built by Metropolitan Cammell at Washwood Heath working the 2.38pm Nottingham to Leicester stopping train passing Trent Junction in April 1958. The DMU service between the two cities was inaugurated during that month. *Joe Wade.*

Route 2 Eastbound – to Nottingham/Lincoln & London via Melton Mowbray

Not the most admired of locomotives and often referred to as 'Flying Pigs', Ivatt 2-6-0 Class '4MT' No. 43016 approaches Long Eaton Junction with the 8.28am Derby-Nottingham parcels train on 2 June 1959. Built in 1948 at Horwich Works and withdrawn in February 1966 from Manningham shed and disposed of at T. W. Ward, Beighton. The line off to the right (Long Eaton curve) going under the high-level goods line is to North Erewash Junction and the Erewash Valley line. *Tony Smith.*

Ivatt 2-6-0 Class '2MT' No. 46499 with an Officers Saloon which has just left Trent station on 2 June 1959 heading in the Nottingham direction. Built in 1952 at Darlington Works and withdrawn from Carnforth shed after fifteen years service and broken up at J. McWilliams, Shettleston. In the background is the Trent Girder Yard. *Tony Smith.*

Ex-GCR 'Large Director' 4-4-0 Class 'D11' No. 62670 Marne is working the 12.10pm Derby-Nottingham stopping train passing Long Eaton Junction signal box on 1 June 1956. Built in 1922 at Gorton Works and withdrawn in November 1960 from Sheffield (Darnall) shed and scrapped at Doncaster Works. *Tony Smith.*

Midland 0-6-0 Class '4F' No. 43860 has the splitting signal at Attenborough Junction for the line to Meadow Lane Junction in May 1957 with a Beeston to Toton mineral train. Built in 1918 at Derby Works and scrapped there when withdrawn in September 1959 from Toton shed. *Tony Smith.*

Little did Joe realise, that he was photographing near Attenborough Junction, one of the oldest passenger 4-4-0s still at work in Britain. Johnson Midland design of 1882 and rebuilt by Fowler from 1909, surviving Class '2P' 4-4-0 No. 40337 seen here with a Sheffield to Nottingham local train off the Erewash Valley line in August 1956. The locomotive was built at Derby Works and broken up there when withdrawn in April 1958 from Hasland shed. *Joe Wade.*

On its way back home in May 1954 is Millhouses-allocated 'Compound' 4-4-0 No. 41062, close to Long Eaton Junction where it will take the curve to North Erewash Junction and calling at all stations along the Erewash Valley with the lunchtime Nottingham to Sheffield stopping train. Built in 1924 at Derby Works and withdrawn from Derby shed in May 1959 and disposed of at Wards, Burton on Trent. *Joe Wade.*

Situated between Long Eaton Junction and Attenborough Junction was Meadow Lane Tip, where Johnson Midland design, 0-6-0 Class '3F' No. 43531 built in 1897 by Neilson & Co rests, having arrived with the regular Monday morning trip from Chaddesden Sidings that also conveyed the sludge tenders. The locomotive was withdrawn from Bedford shed in October 1959 and disposed of at Derby Works. *Joe Wade.*

'Jubilee' 4-6-0 Class '6P' No. 45618 *New Hebrides* now well into its stride between Long Eaton Junction and Attenborough Junction on a winters morning in January 1955 with a Manchester (Central) to London (St Pancras) express, running via Nottingham and Melton Mowbray. Built in 1934 at Crewe Works and withdrawn in February 1964 from Burton shed and broken up at A. Looms, Spondon. *Joe Wade.*

Built at Darlington Works in 1952, and lasting barely fifteen years before its withdrawal from Aintree shed and cut up at T. W. Ward, Killamarsh. Ivatt 2-6-0 Class '2' No. 46502 is on a local stopping train from Nottingham approaching Long Eaton Junction in August 1956. *Joe Wade.*

Hughes 2-6-0 'Crab' Class '6P5F' No. 42784 built at Crewe Works in 1927, with others of the class referred to as Horwich 'Mogul', is approaching Long Eaton Junction in August 1956 with an excursion train heading for the stations down the Erewash Valley line. These locomotives being ideal for excursion and holiday traffic when not used for freight work. Built in 1927 at Crewe Works and withdrawn from Saltley shed at the end of 1962 and disposed of at Derby Works. *Joe Wade.*

Running bunker first, Fairburn 2-6-4T Class '4P' No. 42133 near Trent with a local passenger train from Nottingham in September 1953. Built in 1950 at Derby Works and withdrawn from Birkenhead shed in April 1967 and disposed of at Cohens, Kettering.The locomotive is still sporting the lettering BRITISH RAILWAYS in full before the adoption of the first logo (1948–1956) the 'Lion and Wheel' (sometimes nicknamed the 'Cycling Lion'), showing a lion standing over a spoked wheel upon which the words 'British Railways' was displayed. The second logo (1956–1965) featured a lion holding a wheel (which gave rise to the nickname 'ferret and dartboard'), sitting in a crown, with the words 'British' and 'Railways' to left and right. *Joe Wade.*

Having served all stations along the Erewash Valley line, Fowler 0-6-0 Class '4F' No. 43959 heads a local Sheffield to Nottingham train nearing Attenborough Junction in August 1953. Built by Armstrong Whitworth in 1921 and allocated to Hasland shed from new and long time resident thereat until condemned in January 1957 and disposed of at Derby Works. *Joe Wade.*

A short lived locomotive, Fairburn 2-6-4T Class '4MT' No. 42182 is working a Nottingham-Leicester local stopping train approaching Trent in July 1956. Built in 1948 at Derby Works had just seven more years left to run when this picture was taken before being withdrawn from Willesden shed and broken up at Crewe Works. *Joe Wade.*

Manufactured by Neilson, Reid & Co. Fowler rebuild of Johnson design, 4-4-0 Class '2P' No. 40553 is passing Long Eaton Junction's starting signal with a local train for Nottingham in August 1956, a couple of years before withdrawal from Nottingham shed and disposal at Cashmore's, Great Bridge. *Joe Wade.*

Ivatt 2-6-0 Class '4MT' No. 43040 with a local train from Nottingham between Attenborough Junction and Long Eaton Junction in September 1953. Built in 1949 at Horwich Works, LMS taper boiler design with double chimney. Later engines built with single chimney, with which earlier locomotives were rebuilt. Withdrawn in November 1966 from North Blyth shed and scrapped by Clayton & Davie, Dunston-on-Tyne. *Joe Wade.*

Liverpool (Edge Hill)-allocated Fowler 'Patriot' Class No. 45518 *Bradshaw* recently ex-Works from Crewe on what would turn out to be its last Heavy Intermediate repair, eases its train for Nottingham over the junction at Trent Station North with the signal set for the goods line to Long Eaton Junction in 1961. Built in 1933 at Crewe Works and withdrawn at the end of October 1962 from Lancaster Green Ayre shed and cut up at Horwich Works. *Joe Wade.*

Often referred to as 'Duck six', Fowler Midland design 0-6-0 Class '4F' No. 44223 heads the afternoon Nottingham to Derby (St Mary's) Class 'C' fully fitted goods towards Long Eaton Junction in September 1953. Traffic off this service would connect at St Mary's Yard with the 4.25pm Leicester to Carlisle goods. Built in 1926 at Derby Works and withdrawn from Nottingham shed in November 1963 and broken up at Cashmore's, Great Bridge. *Joe Wade.*

Hughes L.M.S. design, a 1927 Crewe Works build under Fowler's direction. Class '6P5F' 'Crab' No. 42761 carrying a Burton (17B) shedplate with a westbound freight from Beeston Sidings approaching Long Eaton Junction in September 1955. Withdrawn from Gorton shed in June 1964 and cut up at Central Wagon Co., Wigan. *Joe Wade.*

A work stained Thompson 4-6-0 'B1' No. 61047 has seen better days judging by its appearance having just passed Attenborough Junction working a Lincoln to Derby semi-fast express in August 1956. Built in 1946 by North British Locomotive Company, Glasgow and withdrawn in September 1962 from Sheffield (Darnall) shed and scrapped at Cashmore's, Great Bridge. *Joe Wade.*

Taken on a hot sunny day in May 1950, an unidentified 4-4-0 Class '2P' rushes through Beeston station with a Nottingham to Derby semi-fast express. *Joe Wade.*

A 1932 Derby build. Post-Grouping development of Johnson Midland compound design, Fowler 3-cylinder 4-4-0 Class '4P' No. 40935 is approaching Long Eaton Junction in August 1956 with an express from Nottingham and with less than eighteen months to run before withdrawal from Bournville shed and disposal at Crewe Works. *Joe Wade.*

Quite unexpectedly in the mid-1950s, five of the ex-GCR 'D11' or 'Director' Class 4-4-0s allocated to the Eastern Region depot at Lincoln began to permeate the Midland lines. The ex-Midland shed at Lincoln had come under the control of the Eastern Region and despite the fact that some LMR engines were still on hand, they no longer found favour on most of the through Lincoln to Derby trains. In August 1956 No. 62666 *Zeebrugge* heads towards Long Eaton Junction with a Derby bound express. Built in 1922 at Gorton Works and withdrawn in December 1960 from Sheffield (Darnall) shed and scrapped at Doncaster Works. *Joe Wade.*

A Fowler Midland Railway design locomotive with reduced boiler mountings built in 1928 at Crewe Works. 0-6-0 Class '4F' No. 44546 is approaching Attenborough Junction in July 1956 having picked up passengers at stations along the Erewash Valley with a Sunday excursion to an East Coast resort. The locomotive ended its tenure in March 1960 from Nottingham shed and was broken up at T. W. Ward, Killamarsh. *Joe Wade.*

Emerged in 1919 from Gorton Works, Robinson-designed 4-4-0 ex-GCR D11/1 or 'Director Class' No. 62660 *Butler-Henderson*, one of five locomotives allocated to the Eastern Region depot at Lincoln (40A) in the mid-1950s. Pictured here working a Lincoln to Derby express nearing Long Eaton Junction on a hot summer afternoon in August 1956. Following its withdrawal in November 1960 from Sheffield (Darnall) shed, 62660 would be preserved by the British Transport Commission and restored to full Great Central livery. *Joe Wade.*

Although Nottingham shed had an allocation of six LMS 'Jubilee' 4-6-0s, 'Black Fives' were also in evidence on the semi-fast workings to London (St Pancras). In August 1953 an unidentified Stanier '5' coasts towards Long Eaton Junction and Trent with an express to the capital. *Joe Wade.*

Transferred from Carlisle (Kingmoor) Shed to Derby some two years earlier, Midland 4-4-0 (3-Cyl. Compound) Class '4P' No. 41143 heads a Nottingham to Derby local train between Attenborough and Long Eaton Junction on a hot afternoon in August 1953. Built in 1925 by North British Locomotive Company, Glasgow and withdrawn in March 1959 from Derby shed and cut up at Crewe Works. *Joe Wade.*

Fowler 0-6-0 Class '4F' No. 44113 plods along towards Attenborough Junction in August 1953 with a train of empty wagons for Beeston Sidings. Built in 1925 at Crewe Works and withdrawn in January 1966 from Westhouses shed and broken up at Cohens, Kettering. *Joe Wade.*

An unidentified Horwich built Ivatt 2-6-0 Class '4' with its motley train of non-corridor coaches working a M714 excursion from Nottingham in September 1953, captured here coasting between Attenborough Junction and Long Eaton Junction. Enthusiasts christened them 'Doodlebugs' or 'Flying Pigs'. *Joe Wade.*

Fairburn development of Stanier design 2-6-4T Class '4P' No. 42185 passing Attenborough Junction with a local passenger train from Nottingham in 1951. Built in 1949 at Derby Works and withdrawn from Nottingham shed in May 1964 and cut up at Crewe Works. The wagons in the background are being unloaded at the Meadow Lane Tip. *Joe Wade.*

An unidentified 'Jubilee' 4-6-0 Class '6P' with Fowler tender getting into its stride a few miles out of Nottingham in the vicinity of Beeston with an express for London (St Pancras) in May 1950. *Joe Wade.*

A gathering of condemned locomotives at Chaddesden Sidings, mainly 4-4-0s and 0-6-0s waiting scrapping at Spondon in September 1959. Two further lines of withdrawn engines are just discernible between the two signals in the centre of the photograph. The line off to the far right behind the locomotives went via Chaddesden and was used by the Midland Pullman to avoid Derby station, and by the 7.35am Nottingham to Bristol express together with the Lincoln to Tamworth 'Mail' to avoid reversal at Derby. The nearby scrap yard of Albert Loom was located to the rear of Spondon Junction signal box where 130 steam locomotives were cut up. *Joe Wade.*

Civil engineering works in progress to replace one of two overbridges at Draycott in May 1959. Metropolitan Vickers Co-Bo 1,200hp units D5701 & D5716 pass the site with a Manchester (Central) to London (St Pancras) express. To facilitate this work, trains on Sundays were diverted over the Castle Donington branch. *Joe Wade.*

Having just left Draycott & Breaston station with a westbound August Bank Holiday Monday excursion in 1953, Stanier 'Black Five' No. 45279 is still blowing off having just gone under the Hopwell Road bridge. Manufactured in 1936 by Armstrong Whitworth and withdrawn in March 1968 from Heaton Mersey shed and cut up at Cashmore's, Great Bridge. *Joe Wade.*

An unidentified Midland 0-6-0 Class '4F' ambles along towards the remains of the closed Sawley station in November 1957 with a goods train from Chaddesden Sidings. Originally named Breaston when opened in 1839, then, to avoid confusion with Beeston, was re-named Sawley the following year. *Joe Wade.*

Westbound express at Draycott in August 1953, hauled by LMS 4-4-0 (3Cyl. Compound) No. 41069 with just two years left in service before withdrawal from Gloucester shed and scrapped at its birthplace Derby Works. Despite work undertaken by the now defunct 'Railtrack', this stretch of line is still susceptible to flooding after prolonged heavy rain permeating from the nearby Risley hills, which then necessitates trains being diverted over the Castle Donington branch. *Joe Wade.*

With a mixture of archaic non-corridor coaches, a Derby to Nottingham local stopping train is on the approach to Sawley Junction station headed by Midland 4-4-0 (3-Cyl.Compound) Class '4P' No. 41144, thirty years old to the day in July 1955. Less than three years later it would be broken up at Derby Works when withdrawn from Bournville shed. *Joe Wade.*

The 4.25pm London (St Pancras) to Manchester (Central) express with twin Metropolitan-Vickers 1,200hp Co-Bo units in charge roars through Draycott in June 1959. To the left is the coal yard and scrap sidings that were shunted daily by the Chaddesden to Sheet Stores trip working. *Joe Wade.*

This 1950 picture taken at Sawley Crossing, where the only illumination was provided by a solitary gas light each side of the crossing as Johnson Midland 0-6-0 Class '2F' No. 58125 heads back to Chaddesden Sidings with the local pick-up freight from Sheet Stores. A Kitson build of 1876 it was withdrawn from Walsall (Ryecroft) shed in November 1955 and disposed of at Crewe Works. *Roderick H Fowkes.*

New from Doncaster in 1954, BR Standard 2-6-0 Class '4MT' No. 76035, still sporting a (14D) Neasden shedplate near to Draycott with the afternoon Nottingham to Derby (St Mary's) Class 'C' fully-fitted goods in June 1958. This traffic then connected into the following Class 'C' Leicester to Carlisle in St Mary's Yard. After a short spell of only twelve years, No. 76035 was consigned to the scrap line at Cashmore's, Great Bridge having been withdrawn from Chester shed. *Joe Wade.*

How brief a working life of some British Railways Standard Locomotives. Allocated new to Leicester from Horwich Works in 1957, 2-6-0 Class '4MT' No. 76086 photographed here in happier times from the fields at Breaston working a westbound freight for Chaddesden Sidings in July 1958. Withdrawn from Croes Newydd shed in September 1966 and broken up at Cohens, Morriston. In service a total of 9 years 4 months and 1 day! *Joe Wade.*

A Stanier 'Black Five' hurtles down the 1 in 1000 changing to 1 in 818 falling gradient approaching Sawley Junction in 1955 before slowing for the Trent curves with a Manchester (Central) to London (St Pancras) express. *Joe Wade.*

This November 1957 picture shows the station house and the platforms at Sawley station where Wilf Baxter and his family were the last tenants. It was originally called Breaston but the name was changed to Sawley to avoid confusion with nearby Beeston. My grandfather was stationmaster there when it closed in 1930. *Joe Wade.*

The fireman of the lunchtime Toton to Chaddesden freight gives a friendly wave to the photographer as his train hauled by Beyer-Garratt 2-6-6-2T No. 47996 approaches Sawley Crossing in July 1955. Built in 1930 by Beyer-Peacock and withdrawn from Toton shed in June 1956 and cut up at Crewe Works. Some fastidious drivers objected to running bunker first and the Toton Local Departmental Committee in 1931 submitted a complaint on behalf of men working the Garratt engines tender first, which was declined by the Company's representatives. *Joe Wade.*

In July 1958 the Midland Division of the London Midland Region secured six British Railways Standard 'Britannia' Pacifics, which, together with a further three later, were allocated to Trafford Park shed. This enabled the Kentish Town 'Royal Scot' 4-6-0s to be returned to the Western Division. Dashing through Sawley station with a St Pancras to Manchester (Central) express in the summer of 1958 is No. 70021 *Morning Star*, the Pacific having only just been released from Cardiff (Canton) shed. Built in 1951 at Crewe Works and withdrawn in December 1967 from Carlisle (Kingmoor) shed and scrapped at T. W. Ward, Inverkeithing. *Joe Wade.*

A little over three quarters of a mile from the old Sawley station is Draycott, renamed Draycott & Breaston station in 1939 owing to the increase in housing locally. This 1958 photograph looking towards Derby has an overbridge in the background, which carries a major road and was about to be replaced by a new concrete structure. The station closed on 14 February 1966. *Joe Wade.*

Despite the influx of six 'Britannia' Pacific locomotives allocated to Trafford Park in July 1958 with a further three following later, and with Kentish Town then receiving a batch of 'Royal Scots' supplementing their allocation of 'Jubilees', the London shed must have been hard pressed for the rostered engine as Stanier Class '5' No. 44690 was appropriated to work 12.25pm London (St Pancras) to Manchester (Central) express, seen here storming past Sawley Crossing in late 1960. Built in 1950 at Horwich Works and withdrawn in August 1968 from Rose Grove shed and cut up at J. McWilliams, Shettleston. *Joe Wade.*

Ex-Great Eastern 'D16/3' 4-4-0 No. 62535 would survive for only another month, seen here leaving Sawley Junction through the thinning mists of an October morning in 1957 with a Derby to Lincoln stopping train. Built in 1903 at Stratford Works and withdrawn in November 1957 from Lincoln shed and scrapped at Gorton Works. Eastern Region locomotives had gradually infiltrated the Midland area in the mid 1950s and this type superseded the 'D11' Directors that had been transferred to Sheffield (Darnall). *Joe Wade*

Ivatt LMS 2-6-0 Class '2MT' No. 46440 is approaching Sheet Stores Junction with a Derby-Nottingham stopping train in October 1957. A Crewe Works build of 1949 and withdrawn in March 1967 from Speke Junction shed and disposed of at Cashmore's, Great Bridge. The footbridge over the Erewash canal leads from Sawley to the factory at Sheet Stores that manufactured and repaired tarpaulins and sheeting to protect loaded open wagons. *Joe Wade.*

Route 4 Northbound - to Chesterfield, Sheffield and the North

A southbound partially fitted freight train with an unidentified Horwich built 'Mogul' with the tender stencilled British Railways on the last stretch of the Erewash Valley line nearing Trent in 1951. *Joe Wade.*

Johnson Midland 0-6-0 Class '2F' No. 58173. Originally built in 1875 by Neilson, Reid & Co. and rebuilt with Belpaire firebox circa 1917. Withdrawn from Toton shed in June 1960 and disposed of at Gorton Works. Photographed in April 1957 returning to the down main line from Claye's wagon repair works at North Erewash Junction. *Joe Wade.*

'Ello, 'ello, 'ello, what's going on here then? Johnson LMS 0-6-0 Class '3F' No. 43650 in undignified repose having derailed as it was leaving the yard. In doing so it has blocked the footpath that ran from North Erewash Junction signalbox (in the background) to Trent station. A Permanent Way Inspector and Locomotive Inspector survey the scene with a re-railing gang on hand. *Joe Wade.*

There's a calamity at Claye's wagon repair works at Long Eaton in October 1959. The tender of LMS '3F' No. 43650 has become derailed at the exit from the siding. Built in 1900 at Vulcan Foundry and withdrawn in October 1960 from Trafford Park shed and broken up at Crewe Works. *Joe Wade.*

Johnson 0-6-0T Class '3F' No. 47223 fitted with condensing apparatus for the London area, seen here shunting Long Eaton curve sidings in October 1956. Built in 1901 at Vulcan Foundry and withdrawn in January 1964 from Toton shed. *Joe Wade.*

LMS 2-8-0 Class '8F' No. 48206 well into its stride at North Erewash Junction after negotiating the second of two level crossings since leaving Toton West Yard with a mineral train for Washwood Heath in April 1955. Built in 1942 by North British Locomotive Company, Glasgow and withdrawn from Speke Junction shed in May 1968. *Joe Wade.*

Shafts of sunlight percolate behind Johnson Midland 0-6-0 Class '2F' No. 58173 receiving attention in one of the three roundhouses at Toton Motive Power Depot in September 1957. Withdrawn from here in June 1960 and scrapped at Gorton Works. *Joe Wade.*

A Bradford (Forster Square) to London (St Pancras) express hauled by 'Jubilee' No. 45639 *Raleigh* passing North Erewash Junction in April 1955 was one of the few trains that didn't call at Trent. The service was later re-routed from Trowell Junction into Nottingham and ran via Melton Mowbray. Built in 1934 at Crewe Works and cut up there when withdrawn from Leeds (Holbeck) shed in October 1963. *Joe Wade.*

Built in June 1927 at Derby Works, Midland and LMS development of Whitelegg London, Tilbury and Southend Railway '79' Class. Pictured here is 4-4-2T Class '3P' No. 41947 on Toton shed in July 1958 and condemned from here in December 1960. *Joe Wade.*

A 1957 Swindon built British Railways Standard 4-6-0 Class '4' No. 75056 leaving Stanton Gate on the Erewash Valley line with a Saturday football extra to Nottingham in 1961. After only 9 years, 3 months, 3 days in service, No. 75056 was withdrawn from Nottingham shed and despatched to Birds, Long Marston for breaking up. *Joe Wade.*

During the war years, and after, Toton was chronically on the block all along the Erewash Valley. Here, in later times ex-WD 'Austerity' 2-8-0 No. 90152 is making good progress on the approach to Stanton Gate with an up mineral train from Westhouses for Toton Yard in 1961. Manufactured in 1943 by North British Locomotive Company, Glasgow and withdrawn in May 1965 from Lower Darwen shed and disposed of at Arnott Young, Dinsdale. *Joe Wade.*

Route 5 Westbound to - Birmingham/Crewe via Castle Donington

The signal box at Lock Lane Crossing was less than two years old when this photograph was taken as ex-LNW 0-8-0 Class '7F' No. 49444 in a deplorable external condition rumbles past with a Beeston to Washwood Heath mineral train on 12 March 1959. Not too frequent visitors to the Trent/Toton area and often referred to as a 'Duck Eight', it had just over two years remaining in service before withdrawal from Edge Hill shed and cut up at Maden & McKee, Stanley, Liverpool. *Tony Smith.*

Although the Castle Donington branch did not have a regular passenger service, it is still used now for diversions when flooding occurs on the main line at Draycott, or during engineering operations. The level crossing gates at Lock Lane have been opened to road traffic after the passage of a Cravens two-car unit working a diverted Nottingham-Derby local train on 27 September 1959. *Joe Wade.*

LMS 2-8-0 Class '8F' No. 48333 in terrible external condition, bereft of a shed plate working a westbound freight from Toton to Washwood Heath ambles along the Castle Donington branch in September 1959. Built at Horwich Works in 1943 and condemned from Bolton shed in July 1965. *Joe Wade.*

New signal box at Lock Lane Crossing nearing completion in November 1957 on the existing site that necessitated a temporary box, (where a cycle is propped up) housing the block instruments. When the new structure was commissioned the crossing gates still had to be opened and closed manually. *Joe Wade.*

With ongoing civil engineering works on the main line at Draycott involving the removal of two overbridges, all traffic was diverted over the Castle Donington branch on Sunday 27 September 1959. On that day Kentish Town-allocated rebuilt 'Royal Scot' 4-6-0 Class '7P' No. 46103 *Royal Scots Fusilier* has just passed Lock Lane Crossing with a London (St Pancras) to Manchester (Central) express. Built in 1927 by North British Locomotive Co. Ltd. Glasgow and withdrawn from Leeds (Holbeck) shed in December 1962 and broken up at Crewe Works. *Joe Wade.*

The first Midland Compound No. 1000. Withdrawn in 1951 from Derby Shed Johnson Midland 4-4-0 (3-Cyl. Compound) Class '4P' No. 41000 and stored at Crewe after 49 years and 8 months in service. The engine was restored in 1959 at Derby to a near original condition and placed in service on enthusiast's specials. Here a Stephenson Locomotive Society Special has just past Lock Lane Crossing on the Castle Donington branch on 27 September 1959, diverted because of engineering works between Sawley Junction and Derby. *Joe Wade.*

The Thames-Clyde Express

The Thames-Clyde Express

Restaurant Car Train

LONDON ST. PANCRAS and GLASGOW ST. ENOCH

WEEKDAYS

				am						am
London St. Pancras	..	.. dep	10 10		Glasgow St. Enoch	..	.. dep	9 20
Leicester London Road	..	.. ,,	11 59		Kilmarnock	..	.. .. ,,	9 59
			pm		Dumfries ..	..	.. .. ,,	11 14
Chesterfield Midland	..	.. ,,	1 3		Annan	..	.. .. ,,	11 35
Sheffield Midland .	..	.. ,,	1 29					pm
					Carlisle	..	.. .. ,,	12 6
Leeds City ..	..	.. .. ,,	2 44		Leeds City ..	..	.. arr	2 26
Carlisle	..	.. .. arr	5 3		Sheffield Midland ..	..	.. ,,	3 38
Annan	..	.. .. ,,	5 35		Trent	..	.. .. ,,	4 44
Dumfries	..	.. .. ,,	5 55		Leicester London Road ..	..	.. ,,	5 12
Kilmarnock ..	..	.. .. ,,	7 11		Kettering ..	..	.. .. ,,	5 48
Glasgow St. Enoch ..	..	.. ,,	7 55		London St. Pancras	..	.. ,,	7 5

A Buffet service is also available on this train

Seats may be reserved in advance for passengers travelling from London and Glasgow on payment of a fee of 2s. 0d. per seat.

British Railways Passenger Services Timetable – Named Trains

'Jubilee' 4-6-0 Class '6P' No. 45664 *Nelson* hurries over the level crossing at North Erewash Junction towards its Trent station stop with 'The Thames-Clyde Express', 9.20am Glasgow (St Enoch) to London (St Pancras) on 9 July 1956. Behind the wall on the left is Claye's Wagon Repairs that originated in Midland days and sold to a rival company in 1937. *Joe Wade.*

One of the highlights of the day in and around Trent was the sight of named trains, such as 'The Thames-Clyde Express' and 'The Palatine'. Pictured here, the train engine, 'Jubilee' 4-6-0 No. 45615 *Malay States* is carrying the headboard of 'The Thames-Clyde Express', 9.20am Glasgow (St Enoch) to London (St Pancras) and has steam to spare now getting into its stride after leaving Trent station in May 1956 piloted by Johnson 4-4-0 Class '2P' No. 40542. The 'Jubilee' was built in 1934 at Crewe Works and cut up there when withdrawn from Burton shed in December 1962, and No. 40542 emerged in 1899 from Derby Works and withdrawn from Nottingham shed with just short of sixty years service and broken up at T. W. Ward, Killamarsh. *Joe Wade*

Leeds (Holbeck) shed, despite having a stud of 18 'Jubilees' on its books, was no doubt short of power on this day in June 1959 as Stanier 4-6-0 'Black Five' No. 44849 deputises for the rostered 'Jubilee' on 'The Thames-Clyde Express' coasting towards its Trent stop. In view of this, a pilot engine would probably be attached at Leicester in order to maintain time. Built in 1944 at Crewe Works and scrapped there when withdrawn in December 1965 from Leeds (Holbeck) shed. *Joe Wade.*

'The Thames-Clyde Express' has just passed North Erewash Junction on its way towards Trent with its customary 'Jubilee' locomotive (possibly 45646 *Sturdee*) minus a headboard in 1951. *Joe Wade.*

The next departure on the clock from this platform is the 12.40pm for stations to Nottingham and Lincoln. Rattling through Trent station, and taking a liberal view of the 15mph permanent speed restriction, is the Down 'Thames-Clyde Express' in the early 1960s, on a very cold day judging by the heavy frost on the trees, hauled, according to David Shaw the Telegraph Clerk, by 'Royal Scot' 4-6-0 Class '7P' No. 46151 *The Royal Horse Guardsman*. It wasn't until 1962 that a Trent station stop was introduced on the Down 'Thames-Clyde Express', thus affording a connection into Nottingham. Built in 1930 at Derby Works and withdrawn from Sheffield (Darnall) shed in December 1962 and scrapped at Crewe Works. *Roderick H Fowkes Collection.*

Clearly showing the rural aspect around Trent station, and with just 119¾ miles left to run to London, 'The Thames-Clyde Express' eases out of the platform on 1 June 1956 on its way headed by Kentish Town 'Jubilee' 4-6-0 Class '6P' No. 45612 *Jamaica* that has worked through from Leeds City. Built in 1934 at Crewe Works and broken up there when withdrawn in March 1964 from Derby shed. *Tony Smith.*

The Shed Foreman at Leeds (Holbeck) had once again borrowed Millhouses 'Jubilee' 4-6-0 No. 45664 *Nelson* to work the up 'Thames-Clyde Express' on a further occasion in July 1956, which is pulling out of Trent station. Built in 1935 at Derby Works and condemned from Leeds (Holbeck) shed in May 1965 and disposed of at Drapers, Hull. A Stanier 'Black Five' is on the goods line (worked from Long Eaton Junction to Trent Station South signal boxes bypassing Trent Station North 'box) awaiting a path. *Tony Smith.*

Freight movements around Trent

Stanier 2-8-0 Class '8F' No. 48271 blasting away lays a trail of black smoke as it rattles over Trent Station North Junction with a Toton-Washwood Heath mineral train on 3 May 1959. Manufactured in 1942 by North British Locomotive Company, Glasgow and condemned from Northwich shed in August 1967. *Tony Smith*.

Coming off the goods line at Trent Station North Junction is Fowler 0-6-0 Class '4F' No. 43955 with the evening 6.28pm Toton to Washwood Heath mineral train on 14 July 1959. Manufactured in 1921 by Armstrong Whitworth and withdrawn in January 1964 from Derby shed and cut up at Crewe Works. Some of the ten railway cottages are visible on the right. *Tony Smith.*

With clear signals through the station Stanier 2-8-0 Class '8F' No. 48272 puts a smoke screen over Trent Station North Junction with a Toton to Washwood Heath mineral train on 24 March 1959. Built in 1942 by North British Locomotive Company, Glasgow and condemned from Northwich shed in March 1968 and disposed of at Cohens, Kettering. *Tony Smith.*

In deplorable external condition, ex-Midland Railway 0-6-0 Class '3F' No. 43735 still coupled to a former MR tender complete with coal rails, traverses the North Curve between Trent Station North Junction and Sawley Junction in evening sunshine with the 6.45pm Sheet Stores to Chaddesden pick-up freight on 14 July 1959. Built in 1902 by Neilson & Co and withdrawn from Derby shed in September 1960 and cut up at Gorton Works. *Tony Smith.*

When Royalty travelled overnight, the Royal Train on occasions was stabled on the North Curve between Trent Station North Junction and Sawley Junction amid tight security, on a need to know basis, the out of the way location being a boon for such things. Here the Sheet Stores trip is on its way back to Chaddesden Sidings meandering along with Midland 0-6-0 Class '4F' No. 44195 on 18 June 1959. Built in 1925 at St Rollox Works and withdrawn in March 1965 from Warrington Dallam shed and scrapped at T. W. Ward, Beighton. *Tony Smith.*

Not long out of the 'shops', Normanton-allocated, ex-WD 'Austerity' 2-8-0 Class '8F' No. 90362 passing the stationmaster's house on the goods line from Long Eaton Junction to Trent Station South Junction with a Beeston to Washwood Heath freight train on 14 July 1959. Built in 1944 by NBL Co. Glasgow and withdrawn from Normanton shed in June 1967 and broken up at Arnott Young, Parkgate. *Tony Smith.*

Johnson Midland 0-6-0 Class '3F' No. 43193 trundles over Trent Station North Junction with a Toton to Washwood Heath mineral train whilst another freight train also from Toton Yard, waits on the goods line. Built in 1888 at Derby Works and disposed of there when withdrawn with just short of 70 years in service from Westhouses shed. The line straight ahead goes to Nottingham and the high-level goods lines are on the extreme right with the ten railway cottages sandwiched in between. Circa 1959. *Tony Smith.*

This photograph, taken from inside Trent Station South Junction signal box of a Stanier 'Black Five' working the 4.28pm Nottingham-Derby (St Mary's) fully-fitted goods, on the rise (1-in-586 & 1-in-220) to Sheet Stores Junction on 25 July 1956. The freight connected at St Mary's Yard into the 4.25pm Leicester-Carlisle fully-fitted train. *Tony Smith.*

An unidentified ex-WD 2-8-0 'Austerity' unusually running tender first, eases its train from Toton Yard slowly over the junction at Trent Station North in May 1959. *Tony Smith.*

An unidentified Fowler Class '4F' 0-6-0 pulls its train off the goods line from North Erewash Junction at Trent Station North in May 1957. The line straight ahead is to Nottingham and the high-level goods lines are on the extreme right, and situated between are the ten railway cottages. *Tony Smith.*

Tony Smith has captioned this train as the 9.08am Toton-Willington power station passing Trent Station South Junction in May 1959 with a Stanier 2-8-0 Class '8F' and its mixture of steel and wooden wagons. In the distance is the brakevan of a freight train going towards Trent Junction that, a few minutes earlier had departed off the goods line from Long Eaton Junction where the photographer is standing. *Tony Smith.*

Midland 0-6-0 Class '4F' No. 44013 in full regulator, putting up a good exhaust as it darkens the sky after recovering from the slack through Trent station, on the up main line with a southbound mineral train from Beeston Sidings in March 1959. Built in 1921 at Derby Works and cut up there when withdrawn in October 1963 from Leicester shed. *Tony Smith.*

One of the most powerful steam locomotive types ever constructed in Britain were the large Riddles-designed BR Standard 2-10-0 Class '9Fs', the last in a series of standardised locomotive classes designed for British Railways during the 1950s. Intended for use on fast, heavy freight trains over long distances, being used on the Toton to Wellingborough/Brent trains and dragging its way out of Toton East Yard in June 1958 we see one of these locomotives No. 92122, with a Brent-bound train of coal from the Nottinghamshire coalfield. Withdrawn from Birkenhead shed with just over 10½ years in service and scrapped at Campbells, Airdrie. *Joe Wade.*

British Railways Standard 2-10-0 Class '9F' No. 92028, one of ten that were fitted with Franco-Crosti boiler and side chimney approaching Meadow Lane signal box in October 1956 on the down high-level goods line, a short hop from Toton Marshalling Yard. New in 1955 from Crewe Works then suffering the same fate as other BR Standard Classes, No. 92028 was the first Franco-Crosti '9F' to be withdrawn in October 1966 after a relatively short working life, before being torched at Cashmore's, Great Bridge in 1967. *Joe Wade.*

All ten Franco-Crosti boilered 2-10-0 '9Fs' were allocated from new to Wellingborough shed. In original form, exhausting steam through its side chimney, here, No. 92024 is on the goods line near Trent working a Toton-Brent mineral train in June 1957. The engine is blowing off and the open cylinder cocks, together with the white exhaust, suggest that it might have 'picked up the water'. Another locomotive which suffered the ignominy of being condemned, again from Birkenhead shed with less than 13 years service and was disposed of at Campbells, Airdrie. *Joe Wade.*

The signalman at Meadow Lane Junction appears to have been returned the home signal to danger somewhat hastily, as BR Standard Franco-Crosti 2-10-0 '9F' No. 92021 powers away towards Trent Junction with a Toton to Wellingborough mineral train in October 1956. Built in 1955 at Crewe Works and withdrawn, again after less than 13 years in traffic from Birkenhead shed and broken up at Campbells, Airdrie. All ten of the Franco-Crosti '9Fs' were withdrawn in 1967 apart from No. 92028, which had succumbed a year earlier. *Joe Wade.*

A very unkempt looking BR Standard '9F' 2-10-0 No. 92016 on the high-level goods line at Trent working a southbound mineral train from Toton Yard in January 1956. Built in 1954 at Crewe Works and condemned from Carnforth shed in October 1967 and broken up at Motherwell Machinery & Scrap, Wishaw. The '9Fs' also proved their worth working passenger trains with great success during the 1950s, adept at fast running despite its small driving wheels, and for a time was a frequent sight on the Somerset and Dorset where they were well suited to coping its tortuous gradients. Peter Townend in his book 'Top Shed', makes reference to a '9F' set to haul an express passenger train, in place of the normal LNER 'Pacific', from Grantham to King's Cross where the speed exceeded 90 mph down the bank from Stoke. *Joe Wade.*

Johnson Midland 0-6-0 Class '3F' No. 43631, passing Trent Station North Junction signal box with a train of empty wagons off the Castle Donington branch for Toton Yard in March 1956. Built in 1900 by Dubs & Co and withdrawn in August 1958 from Staveley shed and cut up at McLellans, Langloan. The signals coming off the north curve are clearly visible. *Joe Wade.*

Beyer-Garratt Class 2-6-6-2T No. 47969, with its distinctive revolving bunker, runs bunker-first with a Clay Cross to Wellingborough train of empty iron-ore tippler and hopper wagons for the Northamptonshire ore fields as it passes Meadow Lane Junction in May 1957. Toton driver William (Bill) Webb revered these locomotives and liked nothing better than running bunker first, where he could sit with his feet up without smoke and steam enveloping the cab and obscuring the sighting of signals. Withdrawn from Hasland shed in August 1957 and disposed of at Crewe Works. *Joe Wade.*

A Leeds District LMS 2-8-0 Class '8F' No. 48274 ambles through Trent station with a freight train in August 1952. Built in 1942 by North British Locomotive Company, Glasgow and condemned from Stourton shed in September 1966 and broken up at Cashmore's, Great Bridge. At the turn of the century there were two rows of trees on each side of the station, and those on the north/west side are extant today, despite the remodelling of the junction when the station closed from New Year's Day 1968 and the building of an industrial estate, whilst those on the south/east side were felled to allow the construction of the high-level goods lines into Toton. *Joe Wade.*

Freshly outshopped from Derby Locomotive Works on a proving run in August 1952, Johnson 0-4-4T Class '1P' No. 58089 of Plaistow M.P.D (33A) waits patiently at Trent on the 2nd Up passenger line for a path back to Derby after negotiating the North Curve. The locomotive would initially have come down from the London end dead in a freight train to Chaddesden Sidings and then tripped to Deadmans Lane to await a berth in the Works. Built in 1900 at Dubs & Co and withdrawn in October 1954 from Plaistow shed and scrapped at Derby Works. *Joe Wade.*

Beyer-Garratt 2-6-6-2T No. 47974 gathers speed on the high-level goods line with a Toton to Brent coal train in April 1956. With only two months left in service when this picture was taken it was condemned from Toton shed and scrapped at Crewe Works, The mighty Garratts would replace a pair of 3Fs/4Fs on the countless coal trains that so characterised the Midland main line. Three of these engines were built in 1927 with a further thirty in 1930 for the LMSR by Beyer-Peacock Ltd. Since 1955 they had been superseded largely by the BR Standard 2-10-0s on the Midland Division. *Joe Wade.*

With Trent station buildings in the background, BR Standard 2-10-0 Class '9F' No. 92077 rattles past on the up high-level goods line with a Toton to Wellingborough mineral train in April 1956. No. 92077 had a shamefully working life of just over 12 years when withdrawn from Carnforth shed and broken up at Campbells, Airdrie. The introduction of the '9Fs' in the mid-1950s had begun to replace the Beyer-Garratts on the Toton to Brent mineral trains as the latter were withdrawn from service. *Joe Wade.*

More used to hauling expresses on the West Coast main line, rebuilt 'Jubilee' 4-6-0 Class '7P' No. 45735 *Comet* at Trent on 8 February 1964 as it delivers some coal to local signal boxes. Built in 1936 at Crewe Works it also found its last duties working on the Great Central line which was a last haven for redundant steam locomotives on their way to the scrap yards. Withdrawn in September 1964 from Annesley shed and disposed of at Cashmore's, Great Bridge. *Roderick H Fowkes.*

A filthy WD 'Austerity' 2-8-0 on a train of Spanish ore from Birkenhead to Stanton Gate, for the British Steel Corporation Works, is piloted by a Stanier 2-8-0 Class '8F' as it heads north past Trent station on the third down passenger line. The line immediately on this side of the train was a through siding, whereas the other two Down passenger routes are between it and the platform. The leading engine is long-term Toton-allocated No. 48672, which had probably only been coupled to the train so that only one 'path' would be required. This was not an uncommon practice hereabouts and was known as 'saving a block'. *Roderick H Fowkes.*

A Nottingham based Stanier 'Black Five' No. 44658 moves away light engine from the up platform at Trent station, circa 1950. Built in 1949 at Crewe Works and withdrawn in November 1967 from Springs Branch (Wigan) shed and cut up at Cashmore's, Great Bridge. *Roderick H Fowkes.*

On the very doorstep was the country's major marshalling yard at Toton. It was a vital nerve centre in the movement of freight, which via the network of tracks around the station was distributed to and from all parts of the country. Photographed here with a coal train from its home base at Toton is ex-Midland 0-6-0 veteran Class '3F' No. 43824 still carrying LMS on the MR tender complete with coal rails trundles through Trent station in 1950. Built in 1908 at Derby Works and scrapped there when withdrawn from Toton shed in May 1951. *Roderick H Fowkes.*

An unidentified Stanier 'Jubilee' 4-6-0 eases a condemned Eastern Region locomotive to a scrap yard through Trent station in 1964. *Roderick H Fowkes.*

'Britannia' Pacific No. 70050 *Firth of Clyde*, fitted with a high-sided tender with a nine-ton capacity and coal pusher, passing Trent on the high-level goods line in 1964 returning light engine to Leicester after working empty coaching stock from Willesden to Heeley (Sheffield) carriage sidings. Built in 1954 at Crewe Works and a victim of modernisation of the motive power fleet, rampant dieselisation resulting in a shamefully short working life of just 12 years and 2 days service before withdrawal from Carlisle (Kingmoor) shed and disposed of at Campbells, Airdrie. *Roderick H Fowkes.*

On the high level goods line at Trent during 1964 is Riddles-designed British Railways Standard 4-6-0 Class '5' No. 73091 working a Leeds-Leicester Class 'C' fully-fitted fast freight. Built in 1955 at Derby Works and withdrawn with less than 10 years in service from Gloucester shed and broken up at Birds, Risca. *Roderick H Fowkes.*

BR Standard 2-10-0 Class '9F' No. 92005 passing Trent on the high level goods line with a rake of fully fitted vacuum braked iron-ore tipplers for the Northamptonshire ore fields. Built in 1954 at Crewe Works and withdrawn in August 1965 from York shed and cut up at T. W. Ward, Beighton. *Roderick H Fowkes.*

'Britannia' Pacific No. 70016 *Ariel* is pictured with a train of empty 40-ton vacuum-fitted hopper wagons, the so called 'Tin Trunks', 'Ghost Train', 'Forty Tonners', from Stonebridge Park power station, on the down high level goods line at Trent. Built in 1951 at Crewe Works and withdrawn from Carlisle (Kingmoor) shed in August 1967 and scrapped at J. McWilliams, Shettleston. The return service ran thrice-weekly from Shipley Colliery, and they would prove to be long-lived with a 8.10pm departure from Toton. *Roderick H Fowkes.*

Hughes-Fowler 2-6-0 'Crab' rated '6P5F' No. 42769 ambles along the 3rd Down passenger line at Trent with a train of empty wagons for Beeston Sidings. Built in 1927 at Crewe Works and withdrawn in February 1964 from Gorton shed and disposed of at Hesslewoods, Attercliffe. *Roderick H Fowkes.*

Fresh off the production line, the last 'Peak' diesel to emerge from Crewe Works in June 1963, BR/Sulzer Type '4' D57 (later 45 042) temporarily up rated from 2,500hp to 2,750hp and on loan to Toton. Seen here passing through Trent with a train of 21-ton vacuum fitted wagons from Castle Donington power station to Langley Mill. Withdrawn in April 1985 and cut up at Vic Berry, Leicester. *Roderick H Fowkes.*

'Jubilee' 4-6-0 No. 45641 *Sandwich* for many years Kentish Town-allocated and then Nottingham, now carrying a Burton (17B) shedplate ambles light engine through Trent station. Built in 1934 at Crewe Works and withdrawn from Burton shed in September 1964 and broken up at Cashmore's, Great Bridge. *Roderick H Fowkes.*

Signalman George Bailey - 'a true Gentleman' - in Trent Station North signal box. He was previously a signalman at Sheet Stores Junction and also Toton Centre where I was his box-lad for a spell in1957. When the Trent Power Box was commissioned in 1969 George was accommodated in Toton Yard as a shunter before resuming signalling duties at Stapleford & Sandiacre.

Passenger sevices around Trent

This is the south end of Trent station, with Immingham-allocated Thompson 'B1' No. 61374 departing for Birmingham with the 7.00am from Cleethorpes on 14 May 1959. The locomotive and coaches would return with the balancing working 4.50pm from New Street. A product from North British Locomotive Company, Glasgow, it was withdrawn from Immingham shed in September 1963 and scrapped at Cashmore's, Great Bridge. *Tony Smith.*

At the north end of the station, Trent Station North Junction box (it dated from the period 1884-1886) looked after the junctions to the North Curve (extreme left), and the Erewash Valley to the left beyond the signal gantry. With its 75-lever frame, it lasted until September 1969. The 12.55pm London (St Pancras) to Nottingham semi-fast departs from Trent station behind Stanier 'Black Five' No. 45342 on 25 July 1956. Manufactured in 1937 by Armstrong Whitworth and withdrawn from Carnforth shed in August 1968 and broken up at Drapers, Hull. *Tony Smith.*

The 11.15am Derby-Nottingham service is approaching, but not calling at Trent station, the signal routing the train over the 3rd Down passenger line. Midland 4-4-0 Class '2P' No. 40676 providing the motive power on 31 May 1956. Built in 1932 at Derby Works and cut up there when withdrawn in August 1957 from Patricroft shed. *Tony Smith.*

Eastern Region Thompson 'B1' 4-6-0 No. 61325 departing from Trent station with the 7.00am Cleethorpes to Birmingham on 4 March 1959. During summer Saturdays, the service was extended to Bournemouth and later to Sidmouth and Exmouth. A freight train from Beeston Sidings stands on the goods line awaiting a path. Built in 1948 by NBL Co. Glasgow and withdrawn from Immingham shed in September 1963 and broken up at Cashmore's, Great Bridge. *Tony Smith.*

Midland 4-4-0 (3-Cyl. Compound.) Class '4P' No. 40929 leaving Trent station with the 11.05am Nottingham-Derby local train in the summer of 1956. The next lines are the 2nd Up passenger then the 3rd Up passenger and the goods line from Long Eaton Junction to Trent Station South Junction, (Trent Station North 'box not involved with that line). On the extreme right are the high-level goods lines to and from Toton. Emerged from Vulcan Foundry in 1927 and withdrawn from Rowsley shed in July 1956 and scrapped at Derby Works. *Tony Smith.*

Just arriving in the station, (signals still in the clear position at Trent Station North 'box), with a stopping train from Nottingham on 11 July 1956 is Midland 4-4-0 (3-Cyl. Compound) Class '4P' No. 41185. Built in 1927 at the Vulcan Foundry it had a further 15 months in service before being condemned from Derby Shed and disposed of at the nearby Works. *Tony Smith.*

A view of the island station with its canopies over the platforms from the Trent North Junction signal box as the 8.07am Derby to Nottingham stopping train departs on 3 July 1956. In charge of the train is Post-Grouping development of Johnson Midland compound design, Fowler 3-cylinder 4-4-0 Class '4P' No. 41095, leaking like a sieve. Built in 1925 at Derby Works and disposed of there when withdrawn in February 1958 from Gloucester shed. *Tony Smith.*

Routed through the 3rd Up passenger line is 'Jubilee' 4-6-0 Class '6P' No. 45654 *Hood* accelerating away with the 8.30am Sheffield to London (St Pancras) express on 6 July 1959, another of the very few passenger trains that didn't call at Trent station, whilst a freight from Beeston sidings stands on the goods line awaiting a path. Built in 1935 at Crewe Works and withdrawn from Newton Heath shed in June 1966 and broken up at T. W. Ward, Beighton. *Tony Smith.*

The lines off and onto the North-Curve are clearly visible as a 3-car Cravens diesel-multiple-unit working the 6.27pm Leicester to Nottingham local service leaves Trent station on 18 June 1959. *Tony Smith.*

The 6.20pm Derby-Nottingham stopping train formed by a cavalcade of Cravens (1X2, 1X2 & 1X3 car) diesel-multiple-units, departing from Trent station on 18 June 1959 whilst signals are cleared on the up line for an arrival from Nottingham. *Tony Smith.*

Coming off the 3rd Down passenger line is Fairburn 2-6-4T Class '4MT' No. 42146 with the 8.28am Derby-Nottingham parcels train on 17 June 1959. Built in 1950 at Derby Works and scrapped there when withdrawn from Derby shed having clocked up just over 12 years in active service. *Tony Smith.*

The 4.54pm Nottingham to Derby local service approaches Trent under clear signals in the charge of Fairburn 2-6-4T No. 42053 on 6 July 1959. Built in 1950 at Derby Works and withdrawn in June 1965 from Trafford Park shed and cut up at T. W. Ward, Beighton. The bridge that the '4MT' has just passed under carries the High Level goods lines over the Nottingham to Trent line, whereas the bridge on the left of the picture carries them over the connection between Long Eaton Junction and North Erewash Junction, the northern side of a triangle of routes. The sidings on the left, which run behind the building, are on the site of the original Derby to Nottingham line, which was truncated with the removal of Platt's crossing in 1862. *Tony Smith.*

Waiting to follow the Nottingham-Leicester diesel-multiple-unit leaving Trent station on 14 May 1959, is Ashford Works 1943 build, Stanier 2-8-0 Class '8F' No. 48620 on the up goods line at Trent Station South Junction with a freight from Beeston Sidings. A member of staff is visible taking refreshment from the water fountain on the platform. *Tony Smith.*

Infiltration by ex-GCR 'D11' or 'Director' Class 4-4-0s in the mid-1950s allocated to the Eastern Region depot at Lincoln became commonplace on the former Midland lines. On 9 July 1956 the 3.5pm Lincoln to Derby express leaves Trent station hauled by No. 62666 *Zeebrugge*. The 'D11s' were later to be replaced by ex-GER 'Claud Hamilton' or 'D16/3' Class 4-4-0s in 1957, before they too were succeeded a year later by lightweight diesel-multiple-units. Built in 1922 at Gorton Works, Zeebrugge was withdrawn in December 1960 from Sheffield (Darnall) shed and cut up at Doncaster Works. *Tony Smith.*

The 3.40pm Derby to Lincoln passenger train was always worked by a 2-6-4T locomotive running bunker first, returning later in the evening (chimney first) with the Lincoln-Tamworth mail. Pictured here is the 7.38am Leicester to Nottingham stopping train with an unidentified 2-6-4T engine running bunker first, leaving Trent station on 3 July 1956. *Tony Smith.*

Tony Smith documented this photograph as 'A special Restaurant Cars express from London (St Pancras) to Derby' seen here passing Trent Station South Junction in June 1956 hauled by 'Royal Scot' 4-6-0 Class '7P' No. 46139 *The Welch Regiment*. Built in 1927 by the North British Locomotive Company, Glasgow and withdrawn from Newton Heath shed in October 1962 and disposed of at Crewe Works. *Tony Smith.*

Considering its importance as a major junction, Trent station presented a sometimes totally deserted picture, but though for most of the time the platforms were bare of passengers, the volume of traffic passing through made it a delight for enthusiasts. The 9.10am Derby-Nottingham stopping train hauled by Fowler 0-6-0 Class '4F' No. 43840 moves off from the station in April 1958. Built in 1917 at Derby Works and withdrawn in August 1960 from Derby shed and broken up at Doncaster Works. *Tony Smith.*

No details of this wintry scene judging by the frost on the sleepers, as Midland 0-6-0 Class '4F' 44472 leaves Trent station with a southbound express in the late 1950s. Built in 1928 at St Rollox Works and withdrawn from Nottingham shed in May 1963 and broken up at Derby Works. A freight train from Beeston sidings is waiting on the goods line to follow. *Tony Smith*

A delightfully clean 'Jubilee' 4-6-0 Class '6P' No. 45655 *Keith* of Trafford Park passing through Trent with a Manchester (Central) to London (St Pancras) express in 1952, again one of the few trains not stopping at the station and running via Nottingham and Melton Mowbray. Built in 1934 at Derby Works and withdrawn in April 1965 from Warrington (Dallam) shed and disposed of at R.S. Hayes/Birds, Tremains Yard, Bridgend. *Joe Wade.*

An 1892 Sharp Stewart build of Johnson Midland design. Rebuilt by Fowler 1912-23, Class '2P' 4-4-0 No. 40411 leaving Trent station in March 1956 with a Derby to Nottingham stopping train. The locomotive was withdrawn in February 1961 after being in service 68 years, 9 months and 1 day, and was scrapped at Albert Loom, Spondon in August 1961. It was just one of the 130 steam locos that were cut-up with at this scrapyard. *Joe Wade.*

Passing Trent Station North Junction signalbox and entering Trent station is Fowler 2-6-4T No. 42330 with a Nottingham to Leicester stopping train in July 1955. Built in 1929 at Derby Works and scrapped there when condemned in December 1961 from Leicester shed. *Joe Wade.*

This is a Fairburn development of Stanier design with taper boiler, Class '4MT' 2-6-4T No. 42686 passes Trent Station South Junction and is entering the station with a local passenger train for Nottingham, in 1950. Built in 1945 at Derby Works and summoned to Crewe Works for disposal after just 18 years, 10 months and 3 days in service. *Roderick H Fowkes.*

A local stopping train from Nottingham passing over Long Eaton Junction (later to be renamed Meadow Lane Crossing) next stop Trent. Circa 1950. The road on the right led to the rifle range, a farm and the station. Would be passengers had to use this route as a lengthy detour when the footpath from North Erewash Junction to Trent station was temporarily blocked to foot passengers owing to the derailment of LMS '3F' No. 43650 in October 1959. *Roderick H Fowkes.*

Sheet Stores Junction

With Trent Junction signal box visible in the distance, British Railways Standard 2-10-0 Class '9F' No. 92059 wheels the 3.05pm Toton to Washwood Heath mineral train over the junction at Sheet Stores on 14 May 1957. Built in 1955 at Crewe Works and withdrawn in September 1966 from Birkenhead shed and cut up at Drapers, Hull. *Tony Smith.*

This was my first relieving point as a Control Reporter – signalbox lad – at Sheet Stores Junction in January 1957. Thompson 4-6-0 'B1' No. 61258 eases a Derby to Lincoln stopping train over the junction in December 1957 and was the last 'B1' sent to Doncaster Works to be scrapped in 1964 having been manufactured by NBL Co, Glasgow in 1947. This is one of many photographs taken by Joe Wade. Indeed, I probably witnessed him on occasions loitering with intent with his lineside permit. *Joe Wade.*

This picture, taken at Sheet Stores Junction in July 1958, shows the 5.05pm London (St Pancras) to Bradford Forster Square express in the hands of Holbeck 'Jubilee' 4-6-0 Class '6P' No. 45597 *Barbados* piloted by Newton Heath Stanier 'Black Five' No. 45101. Double heading on the Midland main line on certain expresses was rife before the acquisition of Class '7P' motive power for the 1957 winter timetable. Long term Leeds resident 45597, built in 1935 by NBL Co, Glasgow and withdrawn in January 1965 and disposed of at Drapers, Hull. 45101, built in 1935 at Vulcan Foundry and condemned from Newton Heath shed in March 1968 was also broken up at Drapers, Hull. *Joe Wade*

The splitting signals at Sheet Stores Junction indicate that the freight from Chaddesden Sidings could be for either Toton Yard or Beeston sidings. It is heading round the south curve towards Trent, hauled by LMS 2-8-0 Class '8F' No. 48644 fresh from overhaul at Derby Locomotive Works in July 1958. Built in 1943 at Brighton Works and withdrawn from Westhouses shed in April 1966 and broken up at Cashmore's, Great Bridge. *Joe Wade.*

Heading south on a Chaddesden to Wellingborough freight at Sheet Stores Junction in August 1960 is Franco-Crosti '9F' 2-10-0 No. 92021, of Wellingborough (15A) shed, the pre-heater of which has been blanked off. Built in 1955 at Crewe Works and withdrawn in November 1967 from Birkenhead shed and cut up at Campbells, Airdrie. The sheet and tarpaulin factory from which the junction took its name, together with a fan of four sidings, is behind the signal box. It produced 10,000 new wagon sheets annually and repaired 90,000 already in service. The photographer is standing on the South Curve to Trent, looking towards Derby, as the train makes for Trent Junction and Red Hill Tunnel. *Joe Wade.*

Local trains had been in the hands of Fowler and Stanier 2-6-4Ts and Midland Class '2' 4-4-0s. The Midland shed at Lincoln had come under the control of the Eastern Region and although a small number of LM engines were still serviced there, most of the through Lincoln-Derby workings were by ER locos. In July 1958 Robinson GCR 4-6-2T Class 'A5' No. 69824 is at Sheet Stores Junction with a Lincoln-Derby train. Built 1923 at Gorton Works and withdrawn from Lincoln shed in December 1958 and disposed of at Darlington Works. *Joe Wade.*

This view, taken from the signalbox at Sheet Stores Junction, shows LMS '8F' 2-8-0 No. 48698 with a Toton to Washwood Heath mineral train in 1959 coming round the south curve from Trent station. It is bound for the Castle Donington branch. Built in 1944 at Brighton Works and withdrawn from Colwick shed in April 1966 and scrapped at Cashmore's, Great Bridge. The line to the right is the main line to Leicester and St Pancras, with Trent Junction signalbox and Red Hill tunnels providing the backdrop. *Roderick H Fowkes.*

The Midland was a railway of distinction. Its signal boxes were of wooden construction, the lower half up to floor level finished in overlapping horizontal boarding, painted, in banana yellow with plum ends and surrounds. The large window frames were white, some opening whilst others were fixed. Identification of the signal box was by means of a name board at either end. Sheet Stores Junction signalbox, where I worked, was of standard Midland Railway design. This view is looking southeast and LMS 2-8-0 '8F' No. 48646 is working a Beeston to Chaddesden freight on 15 July 1964 off the south curve from Trent station. Emerged in 1943 from Brighton Works and condemned from Lostock Hall shed in June 1968. The line to the right is from Leicester. *Roderick H Fowkes.*

The gradient from Trent South to Sheet Stores rising at 1-in-586, changing t 1-in-220, although not particularly steep was sufficient to cause difficulty if an engine started slipping. The 15mph restriction through Trent station and the more severe 10mph over Sheet Stores Junction, over which this train is passing, was always a hindrance to the progress of a heavy coal train. Here an unidentified Stanier 2-6-0 Class '6P5F' approaches the signalbox on a very wet day in 1959 with a trainload of pipes from the British Steel Corporation Stanton Ironworks to Washwood Heath. *Roderick H Fowkes.*

A view of a grimy LMS 2-8-0 Class '8F' 48698, it has a clear road going onto the Castle Donington branch at Sheet Stores Junction, which diverges left from the Leicester to Derby line with a Toton to Washwood Heath mineral train in 1959. Built in 1944 at Brighton Works and withdrawn from Colwick shed in April 1966 and scrapped at Cashmore's, Great Bridge. Part of the Sheet Stores factory, from which the junction took its name is visible on the down side. *Roderick H Fowkes.*

The awesome power of this magnificent, majestic Beyer-Garratt 2-6-6-2T No. 47991 is evident in all its splendour captured here with steam to spare after negotiating the final 1-in-220 rising gradient from Trent station to Sheet Stores Junction. However, perhaps all is not well, the driver is looking back and that could be the fireman walking alongside the train which has just run onto the Castle Donington branch with a Toton-Washwood Heath mineral train in this undated picture. Built in 1930 by Beyer-Peacock and condemned from Toton shed in December 1955 and disposed of at Crewe Works. *Photograph courtesy of the late Claude Cook.*

Brand new from the Brush Works at Loughborough in April 1965, Co-Co diesel electric 2,750hp locomotive D1836 (renumbered 47355, 47391 and again 47355 – stored at Carnforth 2010), runs through Trent station with a returning test train of empty coaching stock from Cricklewood to Derby Etches Park.

Electro-diesels E6024 (73118) and E6022 (73210) may seem a long way from home at Trent but, in reality, they hadn't reached home. After construction at Vulcan Foundry, the Type JBs were despatched to Derby for acceptance testing. This is another 'delivery run' in 1965 coming off the North Curve.

This is the 'North Curve' at Trent Station North Junction looking towards Sawley Junction where on occasions the Royal Train would stable overnight. *Photographed by George Bailey.*

Two views of Trent station in the mid 1960s taken by signalman George Bailey. With its solitary island platform that was bi-directionally signalled, Trent was a station without a town. Both photographs were taken from the north-east end of the station and show the Up side platform, looking towards the signal box at Trent Station South Jct. where the lines deviated to Leicester and the South Curve to Sheet Stores Junction and Derby. All peaceful and quiet at Trent, in its heyday during each 24 hours nearly 100 passenger and parcels trains called at the station.

A photograph of the 3.45pm departure from Nottingham Midland station, the 'Midland Pullman' taken by George Bailey, Trent Station North Junction signalman. Heading for London (St Pancras), from where it would form the 6.10pm departure to Manchester (Central), it is seen here going through the Up 3rd passenger line at Trent.

A view of the weir which broke in 1953, taken from the top of Red Hill tunnel in 1964. Weirs were constructed downstream to protect the base of such bridges from the undermining effects of scour in the sometimes ferocious currents so that the water flowed more evenly around the piers, and at a relatively constant depth. Protected by a pile of boulders, the water, where it actually flowed around the base was slower and more tranquil than at the surface, and the piers were never undermined. Owing to the failure of the Midland weir, the River Trent was effectively drained for several feet resulting in the ancient foundations being exposed for the first time since they were built.

George Bailey, signalman at Trent Station North Junction took this undated picture of Highland Railway Jones Goods Class 103 passing through the station. Built by Sharp, Stewart and Co. in 1894 and set aside for preservation by the LMS in 1934, it was restored by British Railways in 1959 and appeared in the 1965 film *Those Magnificent Men in their Flying Machines*. It is now housed inside Glasgow's Riverside Museum.

Demolition of Trent station, a photograph by George Bailey. Trent station closed on 1 January 1968. Shortly after, the bulldozers moved in and the station buildings were razed to make way for track remodelling in conjunction with the new panel signalbox, which opened in 1969 and in 2010 had most of its panel operations transferred to a new installation at Derby.

BRC&W No. D5385 later re-numbered 27036 and transferred to the Scottish Region, passing Trent station on the 3rd Down passenger line with a raft of empty wagons for Beeston Sidings in 1963. Withdrawn in April 1986 and scrapped by Vic Berry, Thornton. To the right of the pylon, in the distance is Sheet Stores signal box.

Brand spanking new from the Brush Works at Loughborough in September 1963 is Type '4' diesel-electric D1542, later renumbered 47430 *en route* to Doncaster. It has been signalled from Trent Station North Junction down the goods line to North Erewash Junction. Withdrawn in February 1992 and scrapped at MRJ Philips, Old Oak Common.

With the sun going down, British Railways Standard 2-10-0 Class '9F' No. 92005 rattles past Trent station on the down high-level goods line with the afternoon Storefield to York iron-ore train in 1964. Built in 1954 at Crewe Works and withdrawn from York Shed in August 1965 and scrapped at T. W. Ward, Beighton.

Seated on a station barrow, this passenger shows no interest at all in Southern Region Pacific, 'Merchant Navy Class' No. 35012 *United States Lines*, despite it being a stranger on the Midland lines. Trundling through Trent station on 12 June 1964 en route Nine Elms to Leeds to work an R.C.T.S. 'The Solway Ranger' rail tour the following day from Leeds to Carlisle. Built in 1945 at Eastleigh Works and withdrawn from Nine Elms Shed in April 1967 and disposed of at Cashmore's Newport.

The signalman at Trent Station North Junction, George Bailey took this photograph of WD 'Austerity' 2-8-0 No. 90650 running light engine from Toton crossing the junction. A product from Vulcan Foundry in 1944, withdrawn from Normanton shed in June 1967 and cut up at Arnott Young, Parkgate. The stationmaster's house is clearly visible, with alongside, the panel signal box under construction that opened in 1969 and was finally switched off after 44 years.

Designed at Brighton, British Railways Standard Class 2-6-4T '4MT' Nos. 80079 & 80080 now both preserved photographed leaving Toton for Crewe with the late Driver Malcolm Paling at the regulator. Both were built in 1954 at Brighton Works and withdrawn from Croes Newydd shed in July 1965.

Almost smell the paint as BR Standard 2-6-0 Class '2MT' No. 78010 winds its way down the 3rd passenger line at Trent with a train for Beeston Sidings in 1964. Built in 1953 at Darlington Works and withdrawn after less than 13 years in service from Crewe South shed and broken up Cashmore's, Newport. The signal gantry at Trent Station South Junction bears testimony to lines already removed.

A returning test train from Cricklewood running via Melton Mowbray to Derby Etches Park passing Trent Station North signal box with a brace of Brush built 'Type 4' Co-Co diesel locomotives D1764 - renumbered 47169, 47581 and 47763 - when withdrawn disposed of at Sandbach Car & Commercial Dismantlers, Motherwell, and D1765 - renumbered 47170, 47582, and 47733 - which was disposed of at EMR, Kingsbury when withdrawn. The train conveyed 20 bogies.

The mid-day (11.20am) 'Midland Pullman' service was augmented from London (St Pancras) to Nottingham from 2 October 1961 after long protracted discussions and bitter union opposition to any extension of Pullman services until the Pullman Car Co. had been fully absorbed in the B.T.C. In this 1964-dated scene Signal and Telegraph staff, Bob Naylor, Fred Istle and Wolf Folds poses for the photographer showing the afternoon Nottingham to London 'Blue Pullman' service taking the 3rd Up passenger line at Trent Station North Junction.

A Blue Pullman unit is seen in this 1964-dated shot at Trent Junction with the 3.45pm Nottingham to London (St Pancras) service. The Midland Railway signal, water tower and crane to the left provide a contrast with the 'modern' lines of the unit.